My Awfully Wedded Life

Jimmy Hyten

SAKURA PUBLISHING
Hermitage, Pennsylvania
USA

My Awfully Wedded Life

Jimmy Hyten

My Awfully Wedded Life

Copyright © 2012 by Jimmy Hyten

Sakura Publishing
PO BOX 1681
Hermitage, PA 16148
www.sakura -publishing.com

Ordering Information:
Quantity sales. Special discounts are available on quantity purchases by corporations, associations, and others. For details, contact the publisher at the address above. Orders by U.S. trade bookstores and wholesalers. Please contact Sakura Publishing: Tel: (330) 360-5131; or visit www.sakura - publishing.com.

Book Cover and Design by Mary Raudenbush
Book Interior Editing and Design by Tracey D'Angelo Brown

First Edition
Printed in the United States of America
ISBN-10: 0984678573
ISBN-13: 978-0-9846785-7-0
14 13 12 11 10 / 10 9 8 7 6 5 4 3 2 1

To anyone who has been in a relationship or marriage, or anyone who has had a ridiculous argument with their significant other.

ACKNOWLEDGMENTS

There were so many people who guided, inspired and motivated me through the process of writing this book. I want to thank my new wife, Jackie, for supporting me. She showed me what it is like to be truly happy, and I am convinced that she is the only person who could make me want to be married again. She is the love of my life. Thank you to my family, Mom, Dad, Christie, Mike, Andy, Sheryl, Katlin, Rebecca, Andrew, Luke and Baby James, for being my support system when things got hard. They all have been my biggest fans. Thank you to my best friend James who has been there since I was fourteen years old. Being a military brat, keeping in touch with friends proved to be a daunting task, but he has been there the entire time. He is marrying my sister and it is a blessing to have my best friend become my brother.

I also wanted to say thank you to Oakley, Hercules and Gatsby. Oakley is my ten-year-old dog who I see as my best friend. I feel like he has always been at my side. Hercules was my baby boy Boxer who always made me laugh and I miss him terribly. He passed away this past year but will never be forgotten. Gatsby is our new kitten that is as lively as ever. I have to thank him for keeping me entertained while editing this book.

To everyone I have listed, I couldn't have finished this without you, and for that, I thank you.

Also, some names in this book have been changed to protect the privacy of those involved in the disintegration of my marriage.

CONTENTS

CONTENTS

CONTENTS

Introduction

The evolution of a husband is stated and diagnosed. Everything is and will be justified.

So, I say to all the women on Earth: Do not try and change us, do not try to control our inner child, and, most importantly, do not try and mold us into the kind of man you wish we were. Chances are, if you find it cute that we sometimes act like an eight-year-old, that's how we are always going to act. It isn't a show to get your attention. It is because we are naturally immature. In fact, most men are very stupid and immature in every sense of these words.

Why is this, you might ask? It comes down to one simple reason: defiance. We get stuck in these comfort patterns during our relationships, we become complacent, and we assume there will never be an end to being together. We stop exercising, we aren't on our best behavior, and we don't care if we leave a floater in the toilet. This is when the butterflies and the insanity of a new relationship end and the entertainment begins.

Every day that I woke up with Carly, I would live this life of complacency. I wish I was making all this up, but there is no need here for invention. I share the patent on fractured relationships along with every other married man on Planet Earth.

Divorced men especially, please pay attention to this part: I AM NOT ANTI-WOMEN. I certainly don't think men are right in everything we do. The blame falls equally on both genders. We are equally to blame for our marital misery. We share the blame equally for lining the pockets of our respective divorce attorneys. We're also equal in our pursuit of sometimes unfair custody battles, financial divisions, and the really, really stupid time sharing of our pets.

Having said that, I don't think men as a whole have really had their perspective in marriage fairly represented by TV shows, books, or music. Too many times, I've seen men portrayed as bad husbands who get their asses kicked by women who take martial arts classes. Or, even worse, like the lovable losers in Judd Apatow movies, men who reach some kind of enlightenment about women being of a higher class than men. Well, I want to share my real and very opposite story of marriage and divorce. And I guarantee it ain't no Judd Apatow movie. Not even close.

Jimmy Hyten

Chapter 1: Rules Were Made to be Broken

Emotional chaos, irrational thinking, and a well of infinite unpredictability—this is the definition of a woman's mind. It will never be figured out by a man. We are much too simple of a creature to understand how women think. It's like teaching a third grader a complex math equation until he has memorized it perfectly…and then he never uses it again. That's how it feels with women. Men think they have them all figured out, but nothing they ever do happens the same way twice. It is like lightning—it will never strike in the same place twice.

Because women are such emotional fucking wrecks half the time, men have to take a lot of what they say with a grain of salt. Women don't know what they want, and even if they did, they wouldn't know how to tell us to get it for them. Women speak in code and that code is hidden sometimes in what they say, sometimes in a bodily expression, and sometimes in their eyes without uttering a single word.

Men's thoughts can easily be deciphered. We think about one to three things at any given time: food, sex, or sleep. I suppose that you can add to this list sports, cars, TV, guns and knives, pooping, and beer. But, the thing is, we usually only think about these things one at a time. It's like taking a donkey and having it read your thoughts while tap dancing in a tutu. Men can do some pretty amazing things, but we are usually rather narrowed with our focus.

When men actually cohabitate with these strange and confusing beings that are called women, they have to focus on a stringent set of rules. I learned them from Carly by trial and error, albeit, mostly from error.

Rule #1: Everything is my fault.

Realize this right at the beginning of any relationship with a woman, and you will avoid endless arguments. I would be lottery-rich if I got a dollar every time that Carly said to me, "You know, things would be a lot easier if you would just understand that I am right about everything."

I wish she was exaggerating, but she truly believed that EVERYTHING was my fault. For example, I could be in a deep sleep and if she couldn't find something to wear for work, it was my fucking fault. I could be in my deathbed, seconds from passing away, and she would blame me for the hospital's snack machine not working. If she was sitting on the toilet and ran out of toilet paper, guess whose fault it was? This guy.

Carly got a poor deal on a used car, and it was my fault. Apparently, I should have been there to negotiate for her instead of at my job. Never mind the fact that she asked me to accompany her on our lunch break to "look" at the car, and not make a decision on buying it. So when she independently made the decision to purchase the car and it turned out to be a terrible move, I should've magically stopped her. Fuck my job, I should've been there to intervene and pull a degree in automotive engineering out of my ass.

Rule # 2: Don't talk about the embarrassing things your wife does around others.

My embarrassing moments are the topic of conversation at almost every one of our family gatherings. All my siblings and close friends attempt to embarrass me, which is fine because I'll fling humiliating shit right back at them. It's all in good fun, and I never take it personally. But when Carly tried to join in on the fun and say embarrassing things about me, I couldn't reciprocate without the fear of being handed divorce papers.

At a family dinner that my sister organized at her house one evening, Carly brought up the fact that, on a dare, I had taken a shit in the cat's litter box when I was a kid. The moment she blurted this out, a mischievous glint filled my eyes. I grinned at her and wound myself up for a counterattack.

"Hey, I am not the one who had gas last night," I began. "I'm pretty sure the dogs weren't even in the room while you warmed our bed up with your farts. So, you can't blame them. Guess there was a huge frog or a trumpet player under our bed."

Her head spun like a dreidel. She wanted to murder me right where I stood, but then she realized everyone was staring at her and laughing. There were too many witnesses. She gritted her teeth at me and walked away.

The car ride home was a different story.

"DON'T EVER DO THAT TO ME AGAIN!!!!!!!" she screamed.

"Do what?" I asked.

"I DO NOT WANT YOUR FAMILY KNOWING WHEN I FART OR TAKE A CRAP! I DON'T EVEN WANT YOU KNOWING!" she demanded.

"What are you talking about? I was just joking. No one cares."

"I care! You don't see your brother talking about his wife like that, or your sister's husband talking to your sister like that, or your dad talking about your mom like that!"

"Well, none of them have embarrassing poop stories like I do," I responded.

It felt as if the entire trip home was a battle royale. We seemed to just go in circles before I realized that everything was my fault and I should've let her look awesome in front of my family and let myself look like a stupid pile of shit.

Rule #3: When your wife or girlfriend tells you she is going on a diet, be supportive, and encourage her.

I think every man has dealt with the touchy subject of his wife or girlfriend going on a diet. It usually starts when somebody makes a comment about their weight. Most of the time, it stems from low self-esteem or self-hatred, which is a common trait of most women. It is a part of that emotional imbalance thing they've got going on. Now, I have no problem with someone who wants to be healthier, maintain their appearance, or lose weight. Good for you. But if your wife or girlfriend mentions ANYTHING about going on a diet, don't listen to one word they say. You can't and won't fucking win with this one.

So what do you do when the dreaded "D" word is mentioned? Be supportive. The end.

Don't ever correct what they eat and don't ever tell them when they should work out. Carly asked me so many times to help her with her diet, and each time I did, I wished that I hadn't. I have slapped cookies out of her hand, crushed ice cream cones, and even went to the drastic extreme of telling her that the ice cream she was eating wouldn't help her thighs. All I really ended up doing with these actions was provoke an angry bull that wanted to do nothing but stomp my fucking face in for my actions. It didn't matter that Carly had asked me to help her because, according to rule number one, everything was my fault.

Even attempting to support rather than supervise any weight loss plans can sometimes turn out to be a bad idea. Carly was surfing the net and came across one of those bullshit lose-weight-fast programs. Her face lit up like it was Christmas.

"I am going to buy this diet program!" she said excitedly, "This company seems to really help you lose weight."

A company that helps you lose weight? I'm *sure* there is nothing in it for them.

"How much is it?" I asked.

Avoiding the question completely, she responded with, "Don't you want me to be healthier?"

"How much is it?" I asked again.

"Babe, I want to look good for you," she claimed.

Her avoidance of my question could only mean one thing: it was expensive, but she wanted to gain my sympathy.

"You already look amazing. How much is it?" I asked.

"It's only fifty dollars, but it's a lifestyle change, you know?"

A lifestyle change? What a load of shit. All that said to me was that it was going to cost us money.

The next day, and fifty dollars later, I was at work and decided to call Carly. She had the day off.

"Hey, how was your day today?" I asked.

"Good, I am just eating dinner."

"What are you eating?"

She hesitated for a moment before saying, "Uh…M&M's."

"What?"

"What's wrong?" She asked while feigning innocence.

"What's wrong is that you just enrolled in a 'lifestyle change' and you are eating M&M's! There goes our fifty bucks. I hope that the M&M's are at least delicious and nutritious."

Carly didn't say anything else. Instead, she hung up on me.

What is the moral of the story? Support her diet, even if she falls off the wagon and you come home from work to discover a frozen chocolate Easter bunny and a bag of M&M's spread all over the kitchen floor with your wife in the middle of it all. Otherwise, you will end up on the ground beside her in a pool of your own blood. Or, even worse, you may be denied physical pleasures for the foreseeable future.

Rule #4: Because women say or do something, doesn't mean we can do it too.

I could probably supply a small country with the amount of clothes in Carly's closet. She is into collecting clothes more than wearing them, as most of her wardrobe still has the store tags attached. Since she could practically go shopping in her own closet, you might think this would have stopped her from buying more clothes. You would be wrong. I have even taken the tagged clothes out of her closet, wrapped them up, and given them back to her for birthdays and Christmas. She never once found out. And still, STILL, she continued to shop like a real housewife of Orange County.

I had decided to do the same thing after one of her typical shopping sprees netted over one hundred dollars in purchased clothes. She proudly showed me what she had bought and acted like it was no big fucking deal.

I lost it.

We had bills to pay, and thanks to her careless spending, we had to adjust our budget so that our monthly expenses could be paid on time. I hadn't bought myself an Xbox Live membership, the pieces I needed to complete our gazebo in the backyard, or my morning energy drinks. And although I am usually not a spiteful person, this was beyond upsetting. So I immediately went out and bought myself that Xbox membership and my energy drinks, but I left out the gazebo parts because those could always be returned. When I came home from my shopping spree, Carly threw a tantrum, screamed at me for buying myself some luxuries, and wouldn't talk to me for three days! I guess it was all right for her to blow our money, but I was an asshole for doing the same thing.

Carly was really upset about my "attempt to spite her," as she so callously put it during her tantrum. Yet Carly was consistently the spiteful half of our fractured marriage. She proved it after three days of not talking to me when I woke up in the middle of the night to find Carly sitting suspiciously cross-legged beside me. She was just staring at me in the darkness, holding our pug Harley in her hands. It took a moment to wake up and realize that Carly was holding Harley backwards and that Harley's asshole was shoved against my forehead.

"What the hell are you doing?" I screamed.

Carly pursed her lips and, frighteningly calm, said "I was thinking about what you did, and it pissed me off. So, I wanted to hear the suction cup sound from Harley's butt on your forehead."

I jumped out of bed and immediately washed my entire face, forehead and all. Carly busted out into maniacal laughter. Then it occurred to me—what else did or would she do to me while I was sleeping?

From that point on, I decided, which might arguably be an unwritten fifth rule, to never allow Carly and I to go to bed angry with each other. NEVER.

AND SO IT BEGINS...

Jimmy Hyten

Chapter 2: Intimacy – Lost, Forgotten or Never Really There?

In a society where the divorce rate is around fifty percent, every married couple faces the same daily challenge of not driving each other to the point of no return. So a little insanity is inevitable, but how you deal with that insanity is the true challenge. Many relationships start off in bliss, but eventually evolve into a state of continuous comfort, or worse, agonizing misery.

In the initial honeymoon stage, it's a continuous fuck fest, followed by spending every minute together. You each have idealizations of each other, which result in a mutual agreement that both of you are absolute personifications of perfection. Neither of you can do any sort of wrongdoing or be held accountable for any of your sins.

Once that luster is gone, both of you transform into actual real people, pockmarked with acne and bad breath in the morning. Like a thick layer of filthy dust, a sense of complacency settles over the relationship. You begin to take your needs into consideration more than your partner's, and you stop trying so hard to impress them. It's at this point that men find themselves wondering why the guaranteed sex that comes with monogamy isn't guaranteed anymore. This triggers arguments and resentment. Consequently, the private criticisms of your partner soon become well documented in public. Before long, you're on the front lawn yelling at each other and being filmed on an episode of Cops.

What the hell happened? Where did the passion, intimacy, and companionship go? Did it get thrown in the garbage can along with your dignity and self-respect? All of those lovely quirks and cute aspects to your lover's personality that you found adorable in the beginning end up being the things you can't stand about that person later on in the relationship.

Take sex as an example. Why is the wife the decision maker when it comes to having sex? Every married man in the western world knows exactly what I am talking about. You find yourself asking permission, or scheduling a time convenient for banging, which is typically accompanied by eye rolling, or "I have a headache," or "I'm sorry, honey, I have to make a Bundt cake." You can beg all you like, but if your begging does bear fruit, you find yourself lying on top of a bored spouse who's praying to God for it to be over as quickly as possible. No wonder married men are the silent masturbation champions!

After growing up with two sisters and a mother, I am well acquainted with the many excuses women claim to not enjoy sex, or would prefer to enjoy it once a month or, God forbid, a few times a year. I have heard excuses women don't have sex ranging all the way from it not being within "scheduled time" to the excuse of if it happens too often, women can't have an orgasm. As a kid, I also remember hearing things like, "It is the sixth day of the week. Don't come in our room tonight" from my parents. And from my sisters, I heard, "I just wanted to shut him up. So, I just let him lay on top of me." From a male perspective, this is pure shit. Even though what my sisters said is rare, if this is your situation, you should probably seek help from a professional, from your hand, or better yet, from a professional's hand!

* * *

I'm left to wonder how we, as married men, have fallen short. All we can do is try to bridge the gap between pleasure and passion. Both seem to be equally important to men and women, but how does a guy make this happen? I was continuously left wondering why Carly and I didn't have sex more often. If I initiated it frequently, I ran the risk of being rejected and being labeled as "that guy" who only wants "one thing". On the other hand, when I tried to discuss our coital drought with Carly, I was accused of never being happy with our sex life. I always thought women wanted a man who was willing to talk about feelings. There was no middle ground and no place where I could just be a good husband who wanted a healthy sex life and not some "pig" or "the typical man" who only wanted to fuck all the time.

I realize there are numerous and varied reasons why married couples don't have sex more often: physical conditions, health reasons, medications, etc. But aside from physical problems, health concerns, and medications, the fact is that most women seem to value intimacy and the closeness to their partner rather than any physical form of love making with their partner. Men, however, are the complete opposite. We constantly want to feel the intense physical joy of having our penises enter into and buried in a woman's vagina. That single euphoric act of physicality is the driving force behind our libidos. It's hardwired into our genetic code. In fact, we can get hard just by looking at a Mrs. Butterworth bottle! That's right. While eating our pancakes and staring at the luscious frame of a plastic woman stuck on a syrup bottle, we're probably also thinking about pouring syrup over a woman's body and licking it off!

Of course, in most marriages (except for a very lucky few) fantasies are fantasies and nothing more. It's a humbling feeling to find yourself firing off knuckle children as you become better and better acquainted with Miss Rosie Palm as your marriage progresses.

...

I am reminded of a story. There was a group of women friends who attempted to keep things spicy with their men. One friend was a mistress, the other was engaged, and the other was a hostess who had been married for twenty years. At lunch one afternoon, the married woman suggested they all surprise their men by greeting them wearing only a black bra, heels and a mask. They all decided to do it and meet back in a few days to discuss their men's reactions.

A few days later, they kept the agreement and met again for lunch. The mistress reported that she went to her guy's office wearing a long and heavy raincoat. Under the raincoat, however, she wore only a bra, heels, and a mask. The mistress flung her coat off and stood in front of the man in his office, completely surprising him. Once he recovered, they had wild sex all night long.

The engaged friend went next. She said she that her boyfriend came home and found her wearing a black bodice, a mask and tall heels. He looked at her and said, "You are the woman of my dreams. I love you," and they, too, made passionate love all night.

When it was the married woman's turn, she sighed and looked down at the ground. Her friends asked her what happened. The married woman said that when her husband came home from work, she met him at the door wearing a black bra, black stockings and a mask over her eyes. He wasn't surprised, nor did he say she was the woman of his dreams. Instead, he walked in and said, "What's for dinner, Batman?"

Jimmy Hyten

Chapter 3: Shopping Pains and the Grocery Gauntlet

Americans are busy people. So busy in fact, that our personal time is something that is both coveted and precious beyond words. So when we Americans aren't required to work, we value time spent on ourselves and take advantage of whatever rest and relaxation is possible in the light of day or dark of night. Yet, as a married man, the time that we spend on ourselves is short lived. That's because our wives have an agenda that we have absolutely no control over! What man would rather go to the grocery store when he can be at home watching sports, taking a nap, having sex, or even playing a challenging, yet singular, game of Twister? On the flip side of this question, why should the wife be the only one who gets to do the grocery shopping?

Here was my dilemma, and I am sure many others would agree with me, I would either stay at home while Carly did the grocery shopping, spending $500 on groceries while buying almost nothing that I wanted, or I would try to control that expenditure by going with her, even though I'd rather be having a root canal or be driving a fork through my eye the entire time. I appreciated Carly because she did spend hours clipping coupons and looking for good deals. But, aside from the savings, all that meant to me is that when we went grocery shopping, it was painstakingly longer than it should have been because we spent what seemed like hours searching through the coupons in the middle of an aisle before we could put something in the cart. For instance, one time Carly and I went grocery shopping at nine o'clock at night to avoid the annoyance of the weekend crowd. While we trolled the store connecting coupons with products, I overheard another couple arguing. The wife was nagging her husband about pushing the cart and getting certain foods. The conversation was becoming intense until I finally heard the husband snort and exclaim, "Look, I'm a guy, I just walk through the aisles. I don't know what I am looking for. I am just here with you!"

When I heard this, I burst into laughter. What he said was absolutely true.

In our arrangement, Carly did the cooking and I did the cleaning. Because of this arrangement, Carly knew exactly what foods to buy. When I was forced to go with her to the grocery store, I was just along for the ride.

So back to our little soiree: up and down each aisle we went, stopping at least four times in every single aisle to look for the fucking coupon items. After an hour and a half of scanning every single shelf in the store, I was so tired that I began whining like a four year old.

"Babe, come on, I'm tired and hungry," I pleaded.

"Fine," she snapped back. "If you want to hurry up and leave, then YOU go to the meat section and you find a good deal!"

Was she joking? I had no idea what a good deal on meat was. Nor did I know what meat she could possibly have wanted! I came to the conclusion that it was time to teach her a lesson! I marched straight over to the meat department to look for the weirdest meats I could find. I was thinking that I could bring back a slaughtered animal's tongue, and, if I could find them, some bull or pig testicles. Chicken legs, liver, animal brains and intestines were also on my diabolical list of "gourmet" meats to search for. With all the giddiness of a schoolboy, I picked up a package of chicken feet and pig hooves and placed them in a plastic bag. Yep, I was feeling pretty confident that I would teach her to never, ever again ask me to buy anything edible, unless it was ordering pizza or buying a case of beer.

Carly walked over with the basket and raised an eyebrow to show her suspicion of what was in the bag. "So genius, what did you end up with?" she questioned.

With the pride of a hunter returning from a successful hunting and gathering expedition, I proudly placed my extraordinary finds in her basket. Picture the black hoofs from a pig wrapped in fat with some sort of bloody juice covering it along with about six chicken feet, also juicy and appearing to have just recently been separated from the dismembered body of the chicken. She stared at me with a look that I thought may have been awe, but in reality, it was her "I've just been "Punk'd" expression. I waited patiently for her reaction. She simply rolled her eyes, turned around, and walked away. She wasn't amused at all.

She should've known better. See, I, like most men, have an uncanny ability to turn into a small child when I am annoyed. But I must admit that I enjoyed watching her deflate like a popped hot air balloon over a large cement field.

As she huffed and puffed away from me and stormed into another aisle, I put my finds back in the weird meat case, but not before splattering my hand with pig hoof juice. Still in my child persona, I shouted; "Look honey, I have pig juice on my hands! PIG JUICE!"

She yelled back, "There is hand sanitizer in my purse, just look for it."

I soon found myself standing alone in front of the weird meat section, pig juice dripping from one hand while I used my other hand to dig through Carly's purse. I felt slightly pathetic and semi-defeated that I'd received little to no response from Carly for my prank. And, as if that wasn't enough, just then a beautiful woman walked by staring suspiciously at me digging through a purse.

Feeling her gaze on me, I stopped, looked at her and said, "What? It's my wife's purse."

She walked away mumbling, "Yeah, sure it is."

The lesson I had thought I'd teach Carly actually ended in my annoyance and embarrassment. Carly returned to where I stood in the aisle, waving ground beef and ground turkey in my face. Of course, it had taken her only a few minutes at the most to find the beef and turkey, but in all fairness, ground beef and ground turkey are much simpler and far more common meats that she initially demanded I find the good deal on.

Not only did I make the trip more miserable for myself, and undoubtedly for Carly as well, I also managed to demonstrate to all the nighttime shoppers how much of a child I really am. My continuing punishment is that, I, like most other husbands, continued to accompany Carly to the grocery store, regardless of how I felt, because the simple fact was that if I didn't, I ended up eating tofu, couscous and prunes instead of steak and hot dogs. But rather than throwing temper tantrums at the grocery store, it had become painfully obvious that I just needed to quietly go where she told me to go and get what she wanted me to get. And if I dared resist, my balls would be crushed, and I would be left with nothing more than pig juice all over my hands.

Chapter 4: Newlyweds - In Love or In Trouble?

I want to talk about the honeymoon stage; the moment early on in every marriage or relationship that demands glorious naiveté from us. It's during this fantastic time that every kiss raises all the hairs on your body. Infractions by either person are met with candles, make-up sex, and lots of phrases like "It's Ok baby," and "I love you no matter what!" All too soon though, reality creeps into this lair of infatuation and pisses all over your burning desires for one another. It becomes perfectly clear once you've decided to be joined permanently to somebody else that you will also be permanently joined to their personal flaws, mistakes, and, perhaps, worst of all, their family and issues therein.

You start sharing a bank account, buying furniture together, accumulating stupid little knick knacks, testing each other's parenting skills by adopting a dog, and even consenting to hang your partner's ugly family paintings on every wall in your house or apartment. Eventually, he forgets to wear a condom, or she forgets to take her birth control pill, and a child is created. Maybe two or three more runts will quickly follow. Somewhere in all of this, that initial stage of innocence is replaced with lingering doubt, dread, and remorse for the fact that you are never going to have sex with another person ever again. All that is left to do is live out the rest of your life paying for a spouse, some kids, a place to live, the dog and, this thought: "What in the world did I get myself into?"

Before you kill yourself or are held responsible for a homicide so heinous it ends up being the inspiration for a Law & Order: SVU episode, know this: These feelings are mutual among couples and are completely normal! Remember, you initiated your marriage or relationship by making a conscious choice to not end up sitting in front of your computer with your pants around your ankles every night. You don't get to choose which part of your life you share. It's all or nothing when you're married. Now don't get me wrong, I'm not saying you can't have your own things or that you have to share everything! It's safe to assume that you will get some alone time when you need to take a shit or watch football. So what happens to the decisions that you used to make by yourself, such as what you buy, how much money you should spend, what you wish to do with it, and pretty much, any other decisions that you used to make in the past by yourself? Guess what, Slick? They're gone.

. . .

A few years back, Carly and I bought a house together. We were newlyweds who lived with her father while our house was being built. If you have ever lived with your spouse's parents, you know what I mean when I say that I would rather have someone stick a fork in my eyeball while getting a root canal before I ever do that again! Her father was under the impression that an air conditioner was unnecessary in the middle of summer in Houston, Texas. He kept the thermostat at a comfortable 87 degrees. The space we were in was about the size of a closet, and if these things aren't enough, we also both felt like we were inconveniencing his life, mainly because he told us daily, "You two are inconveniencing my life."

We lived with her father for the first two months of our marriage, and, because of the difference in lifestyles between Carly's father and us, we would have been more comfortable and more welcome in a Huntsville prison.

The day finally came when we were able to move in to our brand new house and be the married couple that we set out to be. We could be on our own schedules, walk around naked, and turn our house in to an icebox if we wanted. The possibilities seemed endless! Surprise!!! It never works out the way you see it in your mind. We found out about each other's spending and saving (or lack thereof) habits. I began to discover that if we had an upcoming bill, it translated immediately to Carly that she needed her wardrobe upgraded before we used the money. We also found out about each other's eating and sleeping habits. The being cute part was over. We were married, and the gloves were off. No longer would she eat a petite salad or a sliver of chicken. She started eating like a fucking linebacker and making desserts like Paula Dean. I quickly realized that she despised me watching TV while she was trying to sleep. Once asleep, she tossed and turned like a gorilla, and, much to my surprise, I found out that women actually do fart.

The discoveries just kept coming. Take shopping for example. One day, I came home from work and there were about fifteen store bags all over the living room floor. I thought that perhaps my new wife had done some grocery shopping, or perhaps we had given shelter to an urban outdoorsman. So, I checked the bags, hoping to find milk, or eggs, or bread, or even fruit rollups. Instead, I found decorations and household items. I found picture frames, curtains that looked like they were ripped off a Vegas hotel room window, candles, and shelving. I was waiting for Bob Villa to pop out of a bag. I was livid! I marched straight upstairs with bags in each hand and confronted Carly.

"What the hell is all of this shit? We don't have money for this!" I yelled.

"What? They're decorative items. They will make the house look nice," she replied calmly as if she was explaining things to a six year old with a learning disability.

Truth be told, I did appreciate her attempt at making the place look like an actual home, but I couldn't justify the cost in my mind. I opened one of the bags and pulled out a giant key. All I could do was stare at the stupid, ugly, enormous, unnecessary key in awe. I plowed through my thoughts, searching for any reason why she felt compelled to purchase the gigantic, fucking key. "Do we have a giant lock that I don't know about?" I asked myself, "Have we moved into the home of Zeus, and this is the key to the front door?"

Her only reply was a half-cracked smile and the patient look that she used when she made me feel like a retarded six year old. She continued to tell me that she knew we couldn't afford anything that she had bought and, at the same time, telling me that there was no way in hell she was returning anything. That was the dominate factor in this financial betrayal that really got to me. We had that stupid key for a long time. It was displayed in our office area. Just looking at that key made me wonder what I had gotten myself into. I would catch myself staring at it sometimes as if its very existence was to taunt me.

You see, during this time period, we were on a very limited income. We had not yet taken the time to sync our spending habits, calculate any kind of budget, or have any type of joint savings. Therefore, talking from experience, I beg you to take my advice. It is imperative that during the initial period of living together, you need to take the time with your spouse or significant other to adjust as a couple. Otherwise, you end up with a taunting decorative key and a living room filled with shopping bags piled high with uselessness.

...

Unwanted big, ridiculous keys aren't your only problem. As the relationship develops, the inhibition to let down your guard goes away. For example, the first four years of my relationship with Carly, I could not go to the bathroom if I knew that she would hear me shit or fart. I also didn't fart in front of her. I was genuinely fearful of her losing interest in me after hearing and smelling my face-melting stenches. Anytime I took a dump, I would instantly turn the faucet on and start singing whatever song came to mind. I was the way with passing gas; I would hold it in until I got bubble guts before I would let her hear it.

But, the inevitable always happens. While living with Carly's father, we had our own room. Due to the sweltering heat indoors, which made it feel like we were living in a jungle, we always had a fan going. One day, after having just eaten a 7-

11 burrito grande, I began to feel gas building up in my stomach. It was so bad that, at one point, I buckled over in pain and felt like a hot air balloon was bouncing around my viscera. Still, I refused to expel any gas. Instead, I tried to stay busy doing menial chores. However, while bending over to clean the floor just in front of the fan, a silent, massive, green cloud suddenly escaped and surfaced right behind me.

"*Oh Shit,*" I thought to myself. "*I let one slip!*"

From the corner of my eye, I noted that Carly wasn't near me at all. She was reading a magazine while lying in bed. I slowly turned to face her and saw no reaction. HA! I had gotten away with it, or so I thought. Seconds later, she turned her face up and stared directly at me. A confused expression appeared on her face and her nose began to wrinkle.

"Do you smell that?" She asked.

I looked around for anything that I could blame this smell on.

I looked around for the dog. He was nowhere in sight. I looked at her and said, "What do you smell, art supplies or something?"

"NO! It smells like a nasty fart or something."

I realized that no lie was going to work. I was right next to the fan, which had blown my fart right into her face. I slowly sighed. "Well, I farted."

She laughed hysterically at me for a good five minutes, covering her mouth and nose as she proceeded to bombard me with all the pillows on the bed.

It took some acquired comfort before getting to that point, but the first time Carly farted in front of me was quite memorable. It was foreign to me because she had never farted in front of me, and, while I realized she was human, I couldn't believe she had done it. We were in Italy on our honeymoon and had just checked into our hotel. It was a very nice hotel, but it was a little outdated. We had just come from eating a magnificent Italian meal, and with it, came a few stomach cramps. Rather than hauling our luggage up eight stories, we decided to take their small and seemingly early 20th century elevator to our floor. We slowly entered the elevator, which was about the size of a wardrobe box, and began our ascent. I suddenly smelled something so pungent and rancid. It was as if someone had just taken a dump directly on my face. I looked around and then my head turned slowly toward my new wife.

She had a huge smile on her face. "You can't even go anywhere because we are in an elevator. You're trapped!" she said.

"Mother of God, how did that come from a human?" I asked.

I was so shocked that women actually fart, and that Carly, who had never farted in front of me, could have punished me in that way. I slowly came to the realization that she was in fact human and not an alien from Venus.

I guess the first time that you pass gas in front of one another is as bad as it's going to get. So, everything from that point on wasn't so shocking. In my opinion, she had just bombed Pearl Harbor, and the war was on. I gradually became more comfortable with farting in front of her, as did she in front of me. There would be the occasional time when it would be particularly nasty for us both. But, it is a good feeling when you can Dutch-Oven your spouse, be proud of it, and her still be attracted to you. This level of comfort in a relationship is nice because you can be yourself in front of your spouse. However, it can absolutely create the potential for boredom in the relationship. Nothing is new anymore. You think you know everything about the person that you had agreed to spend the rest of your life with. There is no longer any mystery. But, being aware of the possibility of boredom is a great defense against it.

Jimmy Hyten

Chapter 5: A Dog Bed or a Dog in a Bed?

According to an article that I read on everydayhealth.com, forty-two percent of dog owners let their dogs sleep with them at night.

Before I met Carly, there was Oakley. One of his favorite hobbies was sleeping on my bed, but he would only do it if I commanded it. I got him when he was just a puppy. So I was able to train him from the start. Being half Dalmatian and half St. Bernard, he was incredibly intelligent. He and I would spend a lot of nights playing hide and seek. I bonded with this dog like no other, and I allowed him to share my bed. He was my best friend and my protector.

After I got married, things changed. I soon found myself with three dogs: Oakley, Hercules, and Harley, two of which are so spoiled that they must, without question, sleep under the covers.

How I came to be the owner of Hercules is, I suppose, worth mentioning. Driving around on a chilly afternoon, Carly and I pulled into a grocery store parking lot and noticed a sign which displayed, "Boxer Puppies." This instantly got Carly's attention. She loved Boxers and had always wanted one. I, too, had always wanted a Boxer, but knowing the amount of work involved with raising and training a puppy, especially the Boxer breed that is notorious for being very playful all the time, I was less than excited.

"Let's just go look at them for a minute," Carly begged.

We were on our way to go grocery shopping, and we had a dinner to get to later that evening.

"Fine, but we need to hurry," I replied.

We pulled up to find there was only one little puppy left. He was so fucking cute. I had to fight the urge to hug the shit out of him, but Carly had no qualms about immediately embracing the pup. She scooped him up in three seconds flat and, while he enthusiastically licked the makeup right off her face, she shot me the perfect look of contentment and exclaimed,

"He is so cute!!!!!!!!!!!! I must have him! I must, I must, I must!!!!"

I chuckled and said, "Yes he is very cute. I want him too. Now, put him down and let's get going." I began walking back to the car, but she didn't budge. I turned around and was met with her stern face.

"I'm serious. I WANT him," she whined.

"Where are we going to get an extra $300?" I asked.

"You know where."

"Oh shit, that's right" I thought to myself. Before we pulled into the grocery store parking lot, I had explained to Carly that I had an extra $300 in my savings account for a rainy day. To Carly however, this apparently meant buying a random puppy from the side of the road. So, that's how Hercules came to be in our lives. He is a wonderful dog, but I'm pretty sure he has applesauce for brains.

Then, along came Harley. A few years later, in the midst of buying our house, I was petitioning Carly to concede to buying a plasma screen TV. At first, she firmly objected, saying that we didn't have enough money for such an expensive piece of electronics. My persistence, begging, and pleading soon broke through her wall of stubbornness. She proposed a compromise. Carly said that she would allow me to get the plasma. I was ecstatic. She then went on to tell me that there was one condition. She had wanted a Pug ever since the age of four. So, if I allowed her to get a Pug, she would allow me to get the plasma.

A Pug, though? I had never been able to stand them. I was also genuinely afraid that it would run into our furniture, as it clearly did into a brick wall. Obviously, that is the reason why their faces are smooshed-shaped, right?

Since Carly was actually willing to compromise, I thought that it was a fair trade. I agreed to get the dog. After all, I figured that while she would be busy cleaning up dog shit, I would get to relax and watch my new plasma TV, yep, definitely fair.

Harley was entertaining, to say the least. She would quite often run a race with herself around the living room. When we first got her, she was trained to pee on newspaper. However, we would go on and attempt to train her to use the outdoors for her toilet. However, in her mind, that translated for her to go to the bathroom anywhere in the house. For example, if Harley was upset at me for any reason, she would directly go and take a shit in my shoes.

Harley loved to sleep in the bed with Carly and me. Now, we owned a California king-sized bed, and Carly typically got fantastic sleep. I, on the other hand, was lucky to get even six hours of shut-eye a night. This is because Harley and Hercules had decided that I was their human body blanket and drool pillow. Hercules, who was already 95 pounds at that point, insisted that when he wanted to sleep under the covers, he would get on the bed, stand near my face, and stare at me until I lifted the covers up. He would then circle me for five minutes while deciding where to lay down. More often than not, he chose the space between my legs. He would then rest his giant boxer head on my upper thigh…every fucking night!

Harley also liked to sleep alongside me, but it was usually not a problem. She was only thirteen pounds, and if I wanted her to move, all I had to do was flick her across the bed.

So anyway, as Carly slept soundly, I tossed and turned throughout the night, all because she wanted the dogs to sleep on the bed with us. This started with Harley, the dog that I agreed to allow Carly to buy so that I could have the luxury of having a plasma TV. I suppose this was kind of an ironic, sick joke. I was usually so fucking tired from no sleep and working all day that I couldn't keep my eyes open to enjoy the plasma TV. During any given night, I woke up with Hercules' enormous ass in my face or his tongue resting on my mouth. You would think that things could have not been any worse, right?

...

Everyone at some point has dreamed about a noise or event that is actually happening as they are dreaming. One night, I was feeling sore from my workout and had asked Carly to massage my body. She did an amazing job. I went to bed so relaxed that I dreamed she was still giving me a massage. In my dream, she started out rubbing my back and shoulders and then moved to my lower back thighs. So...it was going to be one of those kinds of dreams.

SCORE!

In my dream, Carly let her fingers find their way over to my dick and balls and began to massage them, stimulating me enough that I could feel myself getting hard and wanting to explode. She then went down on me and started licking my balls profusely. In the case that Carly was actually down below sucking my boys, I immediately woke up. While my eyes were adjusting to the darkness, I smiled and reached down to touch Carly so she would know I was up and ready to go. Only instead of feeling Carly, my hands rested on two floppy, furry ears. I realized that Carly was on the opposite side of the bed and it was Hercules that was in between my legs instead! His tongue was all over my junk, creating a drool puddle of pure canine ecstasy in between my legs! I jumped up in disgust.

Carly, startled, woke up and yelled, "What?! What is it?! What is going on?!"

"Hercules was licking my balls!" I yelled.

To this day, I am still amazed that Carly could wake up from a dead sleep (a state she most often was in since she didn't have a monster between her legs… or a dog), gain full consciousness in a split second, realize what was going on, and laugh as hard as she did. To me, it was instantaneous. I jumped up in disgust, and the next thing I saw was Carly laughing hysterically at my midnight misfortune. I have to admit, it is a sobering experience to have the family dog licking your cock and balls.

Yet, nothing changed. Hercules continued to sleep with us under the covers whenever he wanted. I still wonder what the fuck was on my pants to have enticed Hercules to lick them so much, but that is beside the point! The entire ordeal brought me to one final and inevitable conclusion: I was not in charge.

Chapter 6: You Can't Find Perfect Anywhere

For the longest time after being married, I developed an impression of Carly in my mind. I envisioned her as the perfect wife. In my head, we would never have an argument, she would go along with everything I asked, and she would never make the wrong decision. And, with her selflessness and all knowing-powers, she would recognize exactly when I wanted to have sex and would not hesitate to act on that knowledge. I think a lot of married men have this misconception. I would frequently find myself annoyed at something Carly had done and instantly conclude that our marriage was not going to work out. When we were just dating, she could do no wrong, but when she was living with me, every fucking thing she did was annoying or upsetting to me in some way. We weren't Kate and Leo, but we definitely were on a sinking ship. We just didn't know it yet.

One night, when Carly and I first started dating, we went out to eat at a favorite of restaurant of ours. It was one of our favorite places to go because the servers knew us, and we would often go to a movie after eating. Since the movie theater was directly across the street, the servers would always ask if we were in a hurry. We were sitting across from each other, enjoying our burgers and beer, when Carly asked me a question about the movie we were about to see. Taking a second to finish chewing my food, I glanced down at my napkin to wipe my mouth and I felt like I had just been shot in the face with a super soaker. I was soaked with what looked like nearly an entire cup of water. I had to quickly piece together what had happened. I realized that Carly asked me a question to divert my attention from what she was about to unleash. All I could think was, "This bitch just shot a cup full of water in my face through a straw." I was in complete shock, my entire head was soaked and all I could manage to say was "…Why??"

She was entirely too busy laughing at me to initially respond. Once she regained her composure, she choked back down a few more whelps of laughter and said, "I wanted to make sure you didn't act like a raging maniac or a small child at the slightest annoyance."

Um…OK. "Was it really necessary to try and drown me and right before a movie?"

"Oh, it was necessary. If you had cleaned yourself off, had gotten up, and slapped the shit out of me, we would have a problem. But, instead, you handled it well."

I semi-understood, and, although still wet and slightly annoyed, I laughed it off. Chalk one up to feminine logic, I suppose. I mean, what did she think that my reaction would be? Did she think that I was going to pick her up by her throat and toss her against a wall? I was just irritated mostly, and all I would have done as retaliation would have been to fill up my own straw and spit assault her right the fuck back!

Hence, I truly believe that the length of any relationship directly correlates to the level of annoyance each person can withstand. I cannot count the number of times that I have heard my friends talk about how amazingly hot someone is, whether it be a movie star or a girl in the grocery store, and think that because of their hotness, they aren't all kinds of annoying. For every hot girl out there, there is someone she drives absolutely nuts.

A lot of my married friends idolize certain women in their lives and expect their significant other to live up to that idolization. Let's pretend I spark up a conversation with a woman I work with, she is attractive, she works out, and she has a lot in common with me. Let us then say that during the course of our conversation, I hear a lot of things I like in a woman and a lot of things that she does that I wish Carly would have done, such as work out more often, participate in some just-anywhere sex, or do certain spontaneous things for her man. I would find myself wishing Carly was just like that woman. This is a very common attitude with so many men, including my friends. So what does it take to accept somebody for who they really are?

...

Partially through our marriage, Carly and I separated. We had been at each other's throats for about six months. Financially, we weren't on the same page, and, when it comes down to it, we couldn't see eye to eye on anything. One afternoon, I broke it to her that I wasn't happy and maybe that a break was what we needed. Emotionally shocked, she moved in to her friend's house down the street from our house. For me, it took being separated from Carly for four months to realize how much I appreciated her. I figured out that a lot of the things that she did that had annoyed me when we were together really weren't as important as I thought they were. I needed to let them go.

When you get married, or move in together, an adjustment period is vital. This will truly test your compatibility and your relationship. Things can't be perfect all of the time. And husbands need to learn to be more accepting of women as the opposite gender. This can be a very difficult thing to do or very easy, but if you want to be in a relationship with a woman, you better figure it out pretty quickly. Otherwise, you are all kinds of screwed.

...

A patience-testing Monday morning rolled around, and I was trying to get ready for work. I had a load of laundry going, I was ironing my clothes for the workday, and trying to get the dogs fed. Carly apparently needed some clothing out of the dryer. I walked past the laundry room and the dryer door was opened. Half the clothes that were supposed to be in the dryer were on the floor, while the other half were hanging out of the dryer!

What the fuck? Did a fucking gnome jump in there, spin around to some gnome techno, and start twirling around my underwear and shirts like they were glow sticks? Yeah, not sure where that image came from, but it's what I distinctly remember thinking when I saw the laundry room debacle.

Irritated, I walked into the bathroom, only to see a knocked-over box of tampons and a hairdryer on the sink. Based on everything that I had witnessed, I was looking for a half-dressed, menstruating gnome with amazing hair.

"Carly! Are you finished wrecking the house? The kitchen is pretty clean, do you want to go run around in there and see what you can fuck up?" I snapped.

"What the hell are you talking about? And, what is your problem?" she asked.

Without hesitation, I replied, "I was doing the laundry, and you dumped clothes everywhere. I just cleaned the bathroom yesterday, and now there are tampons on the floor and in the sink along with Chewbacca trying to crawl out of our drain."

I think she quickly realized why I was frustrated, and, at the same time, I realized that she would soon be late for work, which would explain her urgency and the tornado of a mess.

Women are definitely not perfect. I think there wasn't a day in my marriage that I wasn't reminded of this fact. Learning to tolerate these kinds of incidents, like the aforementioned gnome rave Carly let happen, is part of living with a female. It also helps to be open-minded. Realizing that even the women who are idolized and lusted over by all men, such as Megan Fox, Kate Beckinsale, and Adriana Lima, (oh and of course, gorgeous big breasted woman in the grocery store), all have annoying quirks that people rarely see. I have no doubt that these women don't think twice about dropping the kids off at the pool while you take a shower, or make you feel the worst degree of guilt for playing Call of Duty instead of sitting on your ass pining for her all day. Life is too short not to find the humor in the small things.

Like gnomes.

Chapter 7: Compromise is A Bicycle Built for Two

Compromise. It's probably the most dreaded word you'll ever hear in marriage other than the phrases, "Not tonight" or "I want kids." Marriage counselors all over the world have declared that there are many important issues in a marriage to ensure its survival: communication, sex, laughter, and happiness just to name a few. But the most important is compromise. Unfortunately for most married men, compromise is a word in a marriage that means that they end up not getting what they want, but their wife, on the other hand, gets everything she wants without exception! What usually ends up happening is that women get what they want because they are sneaky, and most men are too dumb to notice. Women make it look easy, too. All they need to do is flash some skin with a grin and we lose to their sexual prowess every single time. Don't get me wrong, I am not a traitor to my gender, but I have been manipulated like any other hot-blooded male has been by their wives or girlfriends. As a result, I have learned a bit how the game is played.

So whenever I heard Carly mention a compromise, I wondered how badly I was going to get screwed. For example, we normally watched TV before going to bed and there were certain shows that we both enjoyed, such as "Lost", "True Blood", and "Dexter". But, what about shows that she liked and I disliked? Ah, this is where I got fucked over every single time. I spent plenty of nights having to watch the dumb fucking female-glorification show "Sex and the City" because I would give in to her pleading and whining about it being "almost over".

"Can you pleeeeaaaaase just let me finish watching it? Then, we can change it to whatever you like," she said with that cute little pouty lip that all women have perfected.

Of course I agreed, and after listening to a full half-hour of middle-aged woman yapping about sex while gulping down one pink alcoholic beverage after another, it was over. I would be so comfortable lying down in the bed that I would end up just falling asleep and not watching anything. Score one for Carly!

It didn't stop there. I got sucked into the "Sex and the City" dick-hating universe. I eventually ended up liking the show. I liked it so much that we owned every season of it on DVD, not to mention the movies. It was at that point when I realized that it wasn't at all a coincidence. It was planned. Score again for Carly!

Compromise? Carly had already decided what our "compromise" would be before asking me if it would be ok to watch "Sex and the City." Every night that "Sex and the City" was on, she waited with patience for me to surrender my manhood and give in to her pleads until I eventually didn't want to surrender anymore. Inside her little head, she made a calculated, manipulative bet that I would end up liking it because SHE liked it and I wanted to please HER. So she got what she wanted, and, as Carly had predicted, I had a newfound interest in a feminine TV series. I still watch that show, too. GAME OVER!

...

Perhaps the most uncomfortable part about compromising for men is that women seem to have the game of compromising all figured out. Before the game even begins, a woman has already created a scenario in her mind about what her husband is going to do for them and how to get them to do it. And, somehow, we always end up doing exactly what they want. The reason is what I alluded to earlier: sex. Women know sex can be used as a reward or a punishment.

Unfortunately it doesn't work the other way around. Most often, Carly and I argued about money or the household chores. One fight in particular that I can still remember was when I had just finished cleaning the entire kitchen. I mean the place was spotless; I washed all the dishes, put them away, cleaned the counters, organized the refrigerator, washed the floors and organized the pantry. A hospital would be lucky to be as sterile as that kitchen was on that day. I ran upstairs to take a shower only to come back down to find Carly making dinner and everything that entailed. Definition: There was shit everywhere. I was livid and did not hesitate to tell her. The argument went back and forth because I cleaned it, but she was making dinner for us. The only thing that I could think of to do was what she probably would have done to me. If she were in my shoes, she would have been so mad at me that she would have punished me by withholding sex from me for the rest of the week. So, I had made up my mind. She had another thing coming to her if she thought that I wanted to have sex with her after what she had done to my pristine, gleaming kitchen. Looking back, it was one of those arguments that wasn't incredibly serious, and was, in fact, rather stupid. Truthfully, after a few minutes, I wasn't even upset anymore. However, as I sat quietly in the living room sulking, I figured that it was time for me to turn the tables on that woman!

I looked at her square in the face and said, "You know, I have had enough. You don't get thiiiisssssss for the rest of the week!"

To my surprise, she laughed uncontrollably, which I couldn't figure out. What was so funny? Maybe it was because she's said the same thing to me a million times before, or maybe it's because men are so shallow that we actually fall for the threat of no sex, as evident by her next statement to me during this fight.

"Honey, if you just let this go, we'll go upstairs right now and have sex."

I contemplated this for a moment. "What?! My devilish good looks and charm isn't enough? You have to piss me off and I have to forgive you for us to have sex?" I asked.

"Do you want to do it or not? Stop being mad and acting like a baby," she said.

Unbelievable! Not only did I have to forgive her in order to have sex, but she wasn't even being nice about it. And what did I do? So, I exclaimed with absolute sincerity to her, "You got it."

I cleaned the rest of the fucking house too. I knew that my "reward" would be having sex with Carly in every way possible, and this idea aroused me to action (pardon the pun). In retrospect, I felt like a dog being trained to fetch, lick, and sit. And that folks, is the fine art of "compromise" in a marriage.

Chapter 8: In-Laws or Outlaws

Most marriages that prematurely end
do so for lots of reasons: cheating, differing
financial priorities, abuse, emotional
disconnection, etc. It may be a surprise to
you that among the reasons that a marriage
ends, in-laws can be a prime motive to
beeline straight for a divorce court. Then
again, maybe it isn't so surprising,
considering how fucking annoying in-laws
usually are!

Before we were married, I dreaded the
initial meeting of Carly's family. I had heard
so many stories about them and I was
excited, yet terrified. With any long-term
relationship, at some point there will always
be the nerve-racking experience of meeting
each other's family. There are several
avenues that this initial meeting could have
turned out for me or for any guy in the same
position. I may have walked away from the
evening wondering if there was a loaded
shotgun pointed at my back, or I may have
gotten an invitation to spend more time with

her family. One of the most important factors is the first impression, which will set the tone for your entire relationship with the in-laws, or, if you are less than lucky, they will be your outlaws.

There are so many horror stories about in-laws and the first meeting, which coincidentally could be the last meeting. I was concerned about how Carly's family would react to me and if they would consider me to be good enough for their daughter. There was also the added bonus of wondering if I met their expectations in terms of being a proper suitor for Carly. The first meeting with the in-laws is a rite of passage for relationships and indicates the importance of the person being introduced. When the term "in-laws" comes to mind, parents are typically thought of, but in-laws can be mothers, fathers, step-parents, brothers, sisters, cousins, aunts and uncles, or even the family hermit. Every single one of them can affect a relationship to some degree.

Carly had two families and those two families have very large and close extended families as well. Throughout our entire marriage, I was always meeting a new person on her side of the family. The variety in her family was incredibly amusing to me. There are the Mormons, the paranoids, the alcoholics, the painters, the bakers, the Quakers, and the candlestick makers.

Her mother was a flower child of the sixties. I have walked into a room and caught her dancing with her arms flailing as if she were mimicking river dance with no music playing.

Carly's brother, who I met when he was 16 and about 5 feet tall, was always trying to be very protective of her, but was on the unfortunate part of the law for the first few years of his adulthood. Among his list of accomplishments are arrests for DUI, theft, possession, and just an overall disregard for anything or anyone.

Her stepfather and his entire side of the family all have lengthy backgrounds to accompany them. I always had a respect for her stepfather, Pete. He was a college professor and, at one point, he worked at the Waffle House to make ends meet. He was one of four brothers and, honestly, if you lined them up with the exception of the bald one, you wouldn't be able to tell who was who. His parents and one of his brothers followed the Mormon beliefs, which was amusing to me on a few levels because that was really the first time I was exposed to that religion. I was amused at the kind of foods they didn't allow themselves to consume and the clothes they had to wear, along with the facial hair they styled on both the men and the women.

Also on her mother's side, Carly had an aunt who has been shunned from most of her family because, in her eyes, her children have always been better than any other children in the family, including Carly.

Carly had yet another brother and a sister from her stepfather, about six more cousins, three more uncles who all have children, and three sets of grandparents.

Her grandmother, her mother's mother, was absolutely the glue for the entire family. She was always calm and collected, and one of the most understanding women that I have ever met. Being a retired psychologist, she mediated so many of the family arguments, but only after everyone had completed their desecration of each other.

On her dad's side, her aunt and her family had to keep up with the Jones'. They let anyone they could know about the new cars they had or the huge house they had just purchased. That being said, they are were the life of the party most of the time and they rivaled an HBO comedy special. In order to show off their newest additions, they threw the most incredible parties and always had an unparalleled amount of food and alcohol. They always had something going on that you could attend and be a part of. If their parties had any less than 20 people, it was considered subpar.

Her uncle should have had a keg attached to his body because the few times that I had met him, he had popped open a beer before 8:00 a.m. Another uncle owned an antique shop, but lived a hermit lifestyle modeled after the Unabomber. Yet another uncle had two kids who didn't speak to him because he denied their existence for the better part of a decade (that normally leads to an award winning relationship amongst family members).

...

Let me provide you with a little background on Carly's father, Tim, so you can get to know him on the level that I knew him on. Her dad was an extremely entertaining guy. During my study of him, I had calculated a list of the loves of his life in the following order: beer, his Harley, his children and, when he chose to have one, his girlfriend. Also, he seemed to get along with small animals better than he did with most humans. When we started dating, to her own detriment, Carly actually lived with him. He was extremely technically gifted and worked in IT. Carly and I would often make dinner and watch a movie at his house. He would normally head to bed really early and, despite his mind numbing snoring, we were left alone. Our "movie nights" would occasionally evolve into us messing around on the couch. Anytime a relationship is new, screwing around on the couch, in the car, in the swimming pool, on a beanbag chair, or anywhere possible is bound to happen. We were so enamored with each other that we would take any opportunity we could to touch each other on the pink parts. In any case, our movie night would quite often end with her in just her bra and panties. I realize that her dad was just in the next room, but we used his snoring as a gauge for getting caught. We never actually had sex, but we did everything but sex right there on the living room couch. For the longest time, her dad would give me looks like I had just broken the law, and I guess I had, his law. I could never figure out why he took so long to warm up to me. That is, until I realized that her dad had little hidden cameras located in spots around the house for optimal viewing. One of these cameras was aimed directly at the couch. It was also motion censored. This abrupt realization came to me when he had asked me to help him move from his rental house to his newly purchased house. I, of course, jumped at the chance to help out and get on the good side of my future father-in-law. The house was almost empty when Tim began taking the wiring from his surround sound down. It was then that I noticed all the little cameras, and I especially took notice of the one aimed directly at the couch. I nearly poo-pooed in my panties. I was stunned. I was positive that he had reviewed the recording and had seen me, on countless occasions and in numerous ways, violate his daughter. I decided that I would never again even touch Carly while in Tim's house. Do you know that feeling some people get when they think they are being watched all the time? Well, I was being watched—all the fucking time.

...

Meeting Carly's mother and stepfather was a whole different experience altogether. Since they lived in Dallas, Carly and I made a weekend trip out of the first introduction, which was also the weekend of her family's annual get-together. We were summoned to a small community of cottages that could be rented out for special events. Her whole family and extended family were there, and everyone either had their own cabin or shared one. The first morning that we spent in the main house, I was awakened at six o'clock because her stepfather was playing the piano as if he were putting on a concert performing for thousands. Every keystroke sounded like thunder. I could hear his fingers hitting the keys and then the associated tune. Was he playing Beethoven's fifth symphony?! To make matters worse, their two large Cockatoos were singing along with the tune! Her mother then decided to join in, adding even more to the off-key wailing. I've never heard anyone sing the words "Good Morning" with such terrible fucking tone deaf bravado and at a decibel level that would embarrass Ozzy Osbourne!

"What the fuck is that noise?" I mumbled with my face in my pillow.

"It's the birds, and my stepdad. Oh God, it's my mom, too. I'm sorry," Carly said in disbelief.

I was convinced that it was a conspiracy to not only wake us up, but to also drive us away from the city for years.

That had just about completed my misery for the morning, and there was no way that I was I was able to get back to sleep. Once we were up, I found the opportunity to tell Carly that we would be getting our own cottage for the reminder of the trip. I would sooner offer to shave Rosie O'Donnell's nether regions than stay another night or morning in that house.

Thinking that I had solved our noise pollution, it was about 8:30 that next morning when I heard what sounded like a very loud, obnoxious little girl singing or yelling. I wasn't entirely sure.

I turned over and looked at Carly when her eyes popped open. I lifted my head up and said, "I didn't know there were any little girls staying here."

She laid there listening for about five seconds before slamming her head back in her pillow and sadly saying, "That isn't a kid, that's my mom, again."

Her mother was roaming around this entire community of cottages, screaming out her "good morning song." Carly did the only logical thing she could think of. She opened the door, armed with a pillow, and clobbered her mother right in the face as she came skipping around to our cabin. That was the end to her singing, for that morning at least...

...

In an effort to meet Carly's entire family, I introduced myself to almost anyone that I came across. I ended up meeting two of her cousins, Samuel and Scott. Because of the shortage of cabins and us wanting our own space, we ended up sharing a cabin with them. The cabin had two rooms that were connected by a joint bathroom.

I should mention that whenever I take a shit, I hate even the thought of somebody being near me! I mean, it's my private time and I don't even like my dogs to be around when I'm toilet dumping. Unfortunately, the shared cabin had very thin walls, and the bathroom door was just a folding partition. It provided no privacy for anything you might do in a bathroom. I may as well have gone in to the community square and invited an audience to watch me jerk off. No. Privacy. At. All.

So what happens to me? Of course, that evening, I needed to shit.

I looked at Carly and said, "I've been holding my bowels all day long. Do me a favor and stand guard. And don't let anyone in here. In fact, turn the TV on so no one can hear anything."

"Fine," she said reluctantly.

I thought that maybe I had done the impossible and guaranteed myself some privacy. But as I was sitting on the pot taking care of business, I heard Carly start talking to someone. Then, I heard nothing. Had my guard left her post? We had had an agreement! I opened the partition ever so slightly and peaked. Sure enough, she was gone. It was right then that I heard her cousins and their parents come in, all of them laughing. They were carrying on about whatever was going on at the time. Oh perfect! My guard ditched me, and now I had a fucking parade walking by.

I am not a power-pooper. I have never had the ability to shit fast, wipe, and run. I am what is known as a "leisure pooper." I sit down, take my time, maybe read a story on eMobo, and, after my feet start to go numb, I consider finishing up. When I heard what sounded like her entire fucking family walking through the front door, panic and frustration swept over me. I had to finish fast. What could I do except push like I was having a baby? Unfortunately it wasn't fast enough.

"How big is the bathroom?" I heard one of them say.

It sounded like a hoard of elephants coming in to the cabin, and I could hear them approaching the bathroom door. To this day, I can still picture the entire scene in my head. It happened so fast. Four of Carly's family members came piling in, two on each side. Out of reaction, I crossed my legs, put one foot on top of the other, and screamed, "Don't come in! You don't want to smell this!"

You'd think they had never seen a guy sitting on the toilet before. They all apologized while laughing and made their way out of the bathroom. I was mad as hell! I was mad at Carly for leaving and mad at her family for barging in on me. I would never do this normally, but the only way I figured that I would feel vindicated would be to make them smell my wrath. They probably would have anyway because of how paper thin the walls were, but I decided to announce my retaliation. Once I finished up, I walked out and I left the door open so they would all be punished for their intrusion. I was hoping the aroma would kill any fresh oxygen in their part of the cabin. I immediately walked over to Carly,

"What the hell?? Where did you go?" I asked aggressively.

"I walked over to the main house. My brother wanted to show me something."

"You realize that four people just walked in on me taking a shit, right?" I snapped.

I could see the grin forming on her face.

"What?! Who walked in on you?" she asked.

"Your cousins and some other people I have never met, and they all smelled my crap. It smelled like rotten baby food. It was disgusting."

Enamored with laughter, she fled to our cabin to question her intruding family members. They were all still gasping for air outside the cabin. Amidst her laughter, she asked sarcastically what they thought of her boyfriend, to which one or two replied by asking what I had eaten. I have never outlived that story.

...

It was a year or so after my shit debacle when we decided to spend

Thanksgiving with Carly's entire extended family. By this time, we were married, and I was going to be introduced to her step-grandparents for the first time. I didn't think much about it at first, mostly because I had already met the rest of her family and realized they were all fucking bat-shit crazy, but then Carly informed me that they were very southern and very Mormon. Did this mean I would be exposed to whole new level of psycho?

"They are just a little weird," Carly told me when she first brought up the fact that her step-grandparents would be attending Thanksgiving.

"Well they are people, right? I mean, they were born here on Earth, right?" I had replied, trying to reassure myself by being positive.

"Of course they are people, but if you haven't been around devout Mormons before, it can catch you off guard." She warned.

"I think I'll be okay. Thanks for the warning, though," I replied nonchalantly.

I wasn't overly concerned with the introduction, but I became a bit more curious.

Thanksgiving arrived and, with it, an entire house in Dallas full of Carly's relatives. I must have said hello to every one of them too—my voice was hoarse within thirty minutes after showing up. The step-grandparents, of course, were the last ones I met. And do you know how people say that first impressions are the first to go? I'm pretty sure I'll fucking remember my initial meeting with Carly's step-grandparents until I'm a grandparent myself!

Moroni, or "Grandpa," was sporting a very long chinstrap beard and no mustache. He was dressed in a plaid shirt and overalls. I suppose I couldn't really criticize Moroni for his Mormon Farmer look. I hadn't shaven in about two weeks due to simple laziness. In fact, it was first thing that Moroni noticed about me, as he came right up, put his arm around me, and didn't offer a "hello" or even a " nice to meet you," but, instead, said in a very southern tone, "Did ya get past the itch on that beard yet?"

"Uh, why, yes I did," I answered matter-of-factly. "I'm Jimmy, by the way."

He ignored my introduction and ushered me towards the couch. He then proceeded to discuss his conspiracy theories with me—FOR A FULL 6 HOURS! He told me how the American government was trying to kill everyone by using mind control and how barcodes and consumer products are actually made to control people. He also told me about how the Nazi regime was actually relocated to the moon after WWII ended and that an attack by them was eminent. The crazy redneck even gave me all these different websites to check out, which he claimed "supported these facts."

"Um, wow." was all I could conjure up to respond with.

"Now, as soon as you check those websites out, you give me a call and let me know what you think. I have meetn's we can go to."

It was just then when I saw Carly out of the corner of my eye laughing hysterically. I glanced in her direction and realized that I was going to have to end this conversation, but how? The only thing that came to mind was a trick that I used to pull on my brother and sister to leave them confused. It was to spout off a bunch of random sentences relating to nothing.

"Well, all of that is very interesting, just don't lick the ferrets."

"What?" he asked.

"Look, if the bridge overlooks the water, which is longer? A rope?" I asked.

When a puzzled look appeared on his face, I got up as quickly as I could and rejoined Carly. For the rest of the night, I stayed glued to her side.

The icing on my in-law shit cake that night was when after this escaped mental patient was done talking to me and I walked over to Carly she said, "Now do you know why I warned you?"

"Oh. Yeah, I sure do, and I would like to thank you so much for laughing at me from across the room. You know he is going to end up talking to his hand for the rest of the night, right?"

For a long time after that day, whenever I was unfortunate enough to be put in the same room as Moroni, my knees buckled from instant fear of being stuck in his conspiracy rumor grinder for countless hours that I won't ever get back.

And to think, this is just ONE of the in-laws I met that Thanksgiving! I found that each person in Carly's family had their own quirks and I have no doubt that in time, one could develop a tolerance for them, but to be thrown into it the way I was left me with a fear of relationship progression in terms of meeting more family members. For instance, Carly is used to her mother's off key morning banter, but I was not sure that I would have ever learned to withstand the nuclear ear shrapnel that came out of that woman's mouth! The same goes with the rest of her family and all their…eccentricities.

Be careful to anyone who reads this and still believes that marrying your significant other is a singular affair. It's more like sharing a jail cell for life, only this cell has about 30-40 bunks in it and you are the new guy. Get ready to share the toilet and touch your toes.

Chapter 9: Kitchen Chaos

Due to a gender role assignment in the 1950's, the kitchen is very often thought of as "the woman's place." However, in recent years, both men and women alike have redefined the gender attachment given to this cooking ground. We now live in the days of stay-at-home dads and powerful women CEO's. Lots of families, however, still practice the women in the kitchen, men in the yard kind of thinking. It's safe to assume very few men will help out in the kitchen unless it is on their own terms. We like being in charge of the entire dining event, be it a meal, a BBQ, or a special night for the wife.

Other than some exceptions, every couple does things differently to maintain and survive in their household. Carly, for the most part, did all the cooking, and I did most of the cleaning. The reason for this was because Carly actually loved to cook. She got all the cooking magazines, recorded Giada, Paula Dean, and the Barefoot Contessa, and loved to experiment with new recipes. Because of this, I spent very little time in the kitchen during our relationship. I found that I was only in the kitchen when Carly would ask me to clean the kitchen, when I had to do the dirty work like picking the guts from a jalapeño, or when Carly was absent or refused to cook for me because I had pissed her off. If I wanted to get on her good side, I would volunteer to help her make something. This always seemed to put her in a good mood, at least until I left a shell in the scrambled eggs or nuked something for too long in the microwave and caused a mess. Whenever I had assisted Carly in the kitchen, it normally ended in her yelling at me for not doing something correctly. She was so precise about the measurements, and if I wasn't perfect, I learned to expect a hailstorm of criticism to come my way. For example, we decided to make lemon poppy seed scones, and I offered to help.

"Okay, what do I do?" I asked her.

"Just follow the recipe in the cookbook," she said.

It sounds simple, right?

Typically, when following a recipe in a cookbook, all the necessary ingredients are written in a column. Next to it are instructions describing what to mix in and when. The lemon scones recipe was no different. I took one look at the recipe, grabbed a big bowl, dumped all the ingredients in it, mixed them up, and in no time I had the batter ready to go.

Carly had stepped out of the kitchen as I did this, but when she returned, I proudly said "DONE!" I felt very accomplished.

"What do you mean you are done?" Carly asked. A look of shock was plastered on her face. "How could you be done? I left for two minutes!"

"I got the ingredients, mixed them together, and I am good to go. Let's put these things in the muffin tin and cook 'em!"

"You truly are an idiot," she yelled, shaking her head. "You can't just mix everything together, you have to mix them the way the directions say to and then combine things! If they taste like crap, it is your fault!"

I was confident that the scones would still taste great. We let them sit overnight. The next morning, we woke up and decided to give them a try. I asked Carly to do the honors. While I sat at the table anticipating her savory reaction, she picked up a scone and took a bite. The minute it passed through her mouth, she stopped chewing and gasped. Chewed-up pieces of scone fell out of her mouth and onto the table. I ignored this, as it wouldn't be the first time Carly acted melodramatic about something I did wrong. I took my delicious looking ball of yum and shoved it into my mouth. What a fucking mistake! It was flavorless, dry, and repulsive. The batter was shit! I pushed the abomination out of my mouth as fast as I possibly could, letting it splatter everywhere.

"I told you so," Carly said, laughing hysterically.

...

Jalapeno poppers—they seem delicious, at least in theory. I normally hate spicy food, especially jalapenos, but when I discovered that jalapeno poppers are wrapped in bacon, filled with cream cheese, and packed in more taste and less spice by undergoing a slow cooking process, I thought I would give them a shot. The process to create these little treats is a delicate one, involving an hour of preparation and an hour of oven time. The end result guarantees an eating experience that some of my friends have called "sampling the snack food of angels."

Carly and I were hosting a dinner party and agreed to serve Jalapeno poppers as an appetizer. The day of the party, Carly was running around the house frantically trying to get ready and was visibly stressed out. I offered to help her with the cooking of the jalapeno poppers. You wouldn't think that making jalapeno poppers is a hard job, but cutting jalapenos in half, scooping out the scorching insides, and then filling them with cream cheese is indeed a truly daunting task. If you have ever cut into a jalapeno, you know that its juice squirts out in all kinds of different directions. It often looks like a murder without the blood.

Carly asked me to cut somewhere between fifty to seventy-five jalapenos in half. I was about half way through cutting all the jalapenos when I came across the Andre the Giant of jalapenos. I mean, this thing dwarfed all other jalapenos. At first, I thought it was a green pepper. I should have been prepared with a maxi pad just to catch all the juice that it would squirt out. Unfortunately for me, I didn't pay this any attention. The minute I cut into it, I was sorry. The jalapeno juice leapt out and drenched my entire face, including one of my eyes. My eyelids reflexively clamped down as tight as possible, but it was too late. The fiery Jalapeno burn of hell infected my eye. The instant pain that I felt rivaled that of a Chlamydia test… allegedly.

"Oh fuck, oh fuck, fuck, fuck, fuck, its buuuurrrnniinnggggg!!" I yelled.

What could I do? I threw my hands up to my eye (as if that would help), ran to the kitchen sink, and stuck my entire head under the faucet. Cold water poured all over my eye and face, but it only temporarily relieved the pain.

"I'm going blind! Someone take my eyeball! IT BURNS!" I yelled.

Anytime I get heartburn from eating spicy foods, I drink milk. It seems to help when I do, so, I figured, maybe it would work for the fireball stuck under my eyelids? I threw open the refrigerator door and grabbed a brand new gallon of milk. Then, I ran back to the sink, leaned over it, and poured the entire gallon of milk on my eye

"Carly, go get the cottage cheese and throw it in my eye!" I hollered while spitting out milk that was leaking into my mouth. I felt that I needed as much dairy to mask the burn as I could get. Of course, Carly didn't comply with my request, but after about three quarters of the gallon of milk, my eye started to feel better anyway. Once I was finished with the milk and water treatment, I proceeded to hold a towel on my eye for about an hour. It was one of the worst pains that I had ever felt in my life. I mean, my eye was reddened and would barely open for about three hours. It was at that point that I was forced into making a pivotal decision. I realized my "help" in the kitchen would more than likely lead to a disaster and would actually do the opposite of its intention. Thinking about the past several times I had tried helping in the kitchen also made me realize that Carly and I just didn't work well together in the kitchen. You put us in a bedroom, and we had no problem, but the kitchen just didn't work. I decided there would be limits to my help. Carly would do the cooking and the preparation, and I would do the cleaning. While I realize that jalapeno poppers are a wonderful appetizer for get-togethers, I decided to no longer participate in their creation. If Carly was stressed out or under the gun in making something, I figured that I could put together a kick ass grilled cheese sandwich—even mini grilled cheese sandwiches for company—but those little poppers were no longer in my realm of responsibility.

Chapter 10: Adventures in Babysitting

At Age 17, I became an uncle. It was my senior year of high school and my sister, Christie, became pregnant and eventually gave birth to a son, Andrew. I had never had that much interaction with a baby before. So, it was something new. Was I thrilled about the damned Teletubbies and Bob the Builder being on TV all day? Hell no. But, was I excited that I would have a young little mind to mold? Absolutely.

Andrew's father was always back and forth between El Paso and Tucson for employment reasons. So, initially, he wasn't in the picture often. It was a culture shock to both my sister and her husband when she had the baby, as it was not necessarily planned. They definitely needed a little bit of an adjustment period. That is where I came in. Uncle Jimmy to the rescue!

Often, I would put Andrew to bed by wearing a giant Winnie the Pooh costume, and I would do my best to entertain him. I have to admit, it was a little fun for me. I had never minded watching him when his mother and father were away because I always felt like it was a good way for me to figure him out. Before Andrew, kids were a mystery, and I was fascinated by their development and the things that came out of their mouths.

From the time he was three until he was ten, Carly would volunteer us to babysit him as often as possible. She knew what he meant to me and she had "baby fever" herself. Neither of us was ready to have kids, and honestly, I wasn't even sure that I ever wanted to. I made that feeling very clear to Carly, which may have been a contributing factor to her baby fever. When Andrew was around, she would get her baby fix. When he would decide to take a shit on the living room floor, or when he would randomly spout off obscenities without knowing what they meant, she could give him back to his parents. I always thought that this type of situation was the best way to have a child.

...

I recall when Andrew had just turned three, I was assigned the task of babysitting him while I was, concurrently, expecting a very important phone call regarding a sales position with a major phone company. He loved watching the ducks that lived in the lake right next to our house, and since it was a hot summer day, I thought it would be a good idea to feed those ducks. We walked over to the lake together, Andrew wearing only a diaper and Thomas the Tank Engine underpants. While feeding the ducks, I noticed a children's bouncing ball floating up to the side of the lake. This was a man-made lake. So, to regulate the overflow, a large drain had been placed next to a ramp leading into the water. That was where I first spotted the ball. My nephew went crazy. He HAD to have that ball. No Problem. Or, so I thought. The ramp leading into the water was like a mini black diamond ski slope, and I was concerned about falling in. I had my phone with me in case I got that phone call that I was expecting. Knowing me, there seemed to be a pretty good chance that, while attempting to retrieve the ball, my dumb ass would fall into the lake. I didn't want my phone to be ruined, so I figured the best idea was to give it to my three-year old nephew.

I placed the phone in Andrew's tiny hand and said, "Andrew, hold my phone as tight as you can. Do not let it go."

"Okay," he replied with conviction.

I was satisfied with how dedicated he was to holding on to my phone. I slid down the ramp as slowly as possible, careful to watch my step so that I wouldn't tumble face first into the water. I made it within an inch of the ball when a loud splash occurred right next to me. I assumed it was a living creature making its presence known, and then I glanced over to my nephew. He was smiling at me, his arms wrapped behind his back, innocently twisting himself. It appeared that it wasn't some lake monster, but, instead, it was my nephew throwing things at me. I didn't think much of it until I realized that he was no longer holding my fucking phone!

"Uh, Andrew, where is my phone?" I asked as patiently as possible, already knowing the answer.

"I threw it in to see if it would float… It doesn't," he responded with a hint of sarcasm.

He thought he had just solved a murder by figuring out that my phone didn't float. He was so pleased with himself for solving the mystery. My entire body began to shake with anger. My lifeline to the outside world was twelve feet underwater. I

My Awfully Wedded Life

grabbed his hand and stormed back to the house.

Once my sister came home, I told her what had happened and she just began laughing hysterically, which only pissed me off more. I didn't say anything to her though. I got in my car and just drove away, imagining a double homicide and me as the blood-smeared culprit. I went to the library to look up what constituted child abuse, and, after a few hours, I had managed to cool down. I went back home. Andrew was waiting for me at the door with a shit-eating grin on his face.

"Hi, where is your phone?" he asked.

"Good question, Andrew, where is my phone? You threw it in the lake, remember?"

"Yeah," was all that he said.

I was pissed again. My mother happened to be nearby and decided to run interference on me before I turned in to the neighborhood lunatic who puts babies' heads on spikes.

"I tried calling it," she said incredibly, "but it wouldn't ring."

"Who did you think was going to answer, Mom, a fish?!"

• • •

99

My sister ended up buying another phone for me that night.

...

Carly volunteered us to babysit Andrew often, which really meant that I would be babysitting. Even after the whole phone debacle, I guess I really didn't mind though. Life was definitely never dull when he was around.

One day, I was talking with a buddy of mine about jerking off. Don't ask me why, guys talk about weird crap. Andrew was spending the day with me, and, of course, he had eavesdropped on my conversation and heard me use the word "masturbate." He pressed me for information on what the word "masturbate" meant. I refused to tell him, let alone repeat the world back to him. If he repeated that word in front of my sister, especially when I wasn't around, I could just imagine the cops showing up at my door throwing around words like "pedophile" or "molestation", which was not my ideal way to spend an evening. So what does the little linguist do? He decides right there and then to start running around the house, screaming at the top of his lungs, "Masturbate me!!!!!!!!!! Masturbate me!!!!!!!!!!!!!"

Christie wasn't thrilled about this, but all any of us could do at the time was laugh about it. In fact, Christie had the same kind of thing happen to her a few months after the masturbation incident occurred. She was talking about blow jobs at the dinner table while my grandparents and parents were there. That is just how our family is. Sex talk is never off limits. Andrew walked in right when she was telling us a story about her friend and her friend's boyfriend. She said, "… and she was giving him a blow job."

Andrew asked what that meant. Christie told him not worry about it because he didn't need to know. Andrew just looked at his mother, sucked in a deep breath, and said, "I want a blow job! I want a blow job! I want a blow job! I WANT A BLOWJOB RIGHT NOW!!!!!!!!!"

It was hard to keep a straight face while disciplining him for saying this.

...

Despite Andrew's tendency to say inappropriate things, I actually enjoyed hanging out with him. We often would go places together, as I would take him along with me to run errands or to go shopping. One evening, right after he had turned five,

Andrew, Carly and I were driving to Wal-Mart. Andrew kept asking me about African Americans. He wondered why they look different from Caucasian people, and I explained as best I could about the concept of race. Carly assisted in my explanation by making a comparison between her fair skin and red hair and someone with a normal complexion is the same difference between white and black people. He seemed to understand as well as a five year old could, but he was still a little inquisitive.

When we got to Wal-Mart, Andrew told me that he had to go potty, so I took him to the bathroom. We were the only ones in there. While I was waiting for him to finish up, an African American man walked in the door. I looked at Andrew and, while still aiming into the urinal, he looked at the man, then looked at me, then looked at the man, then looked at me once more.

"Jimmy?" he said.

OH FUCKING SHIT!!! Please for the love of God don't ask me anything about the racial differences between him and us!

I immediately covered his mouth so whatever he was saying would not offend the man using the bathroom. The African American guy didn't pay him or me any attention. My nephew tried to ask a question, but I managed to muzzle him pretty well. Once the man left the bathroom, I asked Andrew what his question was, and he replied, "Can I poop in the urinal?"

After we left the bathroom, I told Carly the story of the bathroom incident while we were in the middle of the grocery store isle. She laughed so hard that she had to sit down. My fear was that he would, in light of his recent inquiries regarding race, ask me something about the "chocolate man." His very first inquiry about African Americans was asking me why a man looked like chocolate. For all I knew, with his recent education, he could have told the "chocolate man" that he wanted a blow job while trying to get me to "masturbate him." I would then have had to explain to the man that he was going through a learning process and that no offense was intended. Fortunately, he was only going to talk about poop.

•••

Reflecting on the previous few months with Andrew, I brought it up to Carly that I was not at all interested in having children. I made it clear that I enjoyed being with my nephew, but the fact that I would constantly have to filter my language and hold on to my precious items made having my own child extremely unappealing. While she saw my point, I don't think she agreed, but since we weren't in a hurry to have children, she just left that conversation on the table for another day.

Chapter 11: Time Apart - A Blessing or a Curse?

Having children is unavoidably going to come up between couples either before or after marriage. I spoke about my sister's son, Andrew, because it captured how I feel about children. For most couples, children are one ingredient for a happy marriage/family, but for some others, not having children is a choice they made in order to be in a happy relationship. Earlier, I made a list of the most important ingredients for a successful marriage. One ingredient was left out. Because of its importance, it must be addressed: spending time apart.

The practice of spending time apart is vital for the survival of any relationship, not just marriages. You either spend too much time apart already, you are suffocating each other and need space, or you have an equal balance of time apart and time together. To discuss this issue with your significant other requires some serious finesse.

When Carly and I first started dating, we spent every second together. This lasted for about three months, and then she started acting subdued and occupied. I thought she was just tired or annoyed, but once a week she would "just need to be left alone." I was unfamiliar with this need for alone time. All that I could think was, "Great, all aboard the crazy train!"

I wanted to continue spending every moment together, and she wanted some time to herself? I suppose when you're infatuated with somebody, it's easy to become confused about your significant other wanting to breathe in a separate airspace from you. It depends on how needy you are. As it turned out, I was fucking needy.

After being together for a year or so, she started hanging out with her friends without me. She would also talk about places she was going to go where I wasn't invited. She went on to tell me that she needed a life outside of me. Why would she need anything other than me? I was the light of her life. I was all she could ever want. I was fucking amazing... or so I thought.

She began spending more time with her friends than with me, which turned me into an insecure dog waiting for his master to come back. I acquiesced to Carly's "life outside of me." I told her that if she needed time away from me, then she could go ahead and take it. I was a big boy and I could handle it. Of course, that was a lie. I was more like a two year old who just pee-peed in his pants and needed a change.

One day, I came home from work during my lunch hour and Carly was at my house. "What a nice surprise," I thought, until I got inside and saw the suitcases. She had just finished taking all of her clothes out of the bedroom closet.

"What's going on? Why are you packing your things?" I asked her.

"I just need to be on my own," she answered, her eyes looking anywhere but in my direction.

When those words came out of her mouth, however, I thought she still wanted a relationship, but just to be less... close. She wanted to move back in with her Dad so she could have her own room and her own space. Looking back on this, I looked like a sad little puppy whose owner just struck him. I had no confidence, and I felt like she defined me.

A couple weeks passed, and we technically were still together, but I soon became to realize where we were headed— Splitsville. I didn't know how to handle the situation because I had already convinced myself that Carly was "The One." I was always happy when we were together, and I felt like we connected on a level that I had never had with anyone else.

Eventually the time came for her to kick my ass out of her life. During one of my routine visits to her place, she calmly explained to me that she didn't feel the same about me as she used to. She told me that our chemistry was gone. It was like acetone on nail polish.

"I just don't feel that spark anymore," she insisted. She then gave me the "It's not you, it's me" speech. Every guy has heard this one, and we all arrive at the same conclusion—it's a pile of bullshit. Just like that, Carly and I were done.

The first month apart, I had so much trouble and wondered for the longest time what I had done wrong. I agonized, and analyzed, and cried. I was angry and hurt. How could she fucking do that to me? I always felt that I was a decent guy. I was easy to get along with. I was even patient with Moroni for God's sakes.

The only way I knew how to cope with the situation was to write about it and to talk to people about what I was going through. That seemed to help me tremendously. Perhaps the biggest reason why I endured through the break-up was because of some advice that an old friend gave me. It proved instrumental to sustaining my sanity. His name is Brody, and he was the eternally single guy. He had been in his fair share of relationships, but he wouldn't make that mistake again. He was confident and direct and that is exactly how I wanted to be.

One evening, I explained to him over a Bud light (my taste buds weren't fully evolved at that point) about my break up.

"Look man, I have a simple question for you. Do you want her back or not?" He asked.

"Of course I do. That is all I have wanted." I replied.

"Then any time you talk to her, pretend like you don't care about her. Make yourself unavailable to her, and let her think you don't give a shit about what she does." He suggested.

"Seriously? I don't think I can do that because I care about her so much." I responded.

"Trust me. If you want her back that is what you need to do. You have to be prepared to let your relationship with her go, and once you have, that is when she will come back."

I was skeptical about his method because the last thing that I wanted to do was to show Carly that I didn't care. Brody had such a unique outlook on relationships. He had been burned once or twice, but everything he had said to me that night made perfect sense. I figured I would give it a shot. The worst that could happen would be that we were still broken up.

I began going out with Brody to the bars around town and just having fun with all of my old friends. I would keep myself occupied. It had been some time since I had really hung out with my brother and my best friend. So, we started having man dates. We went to the movies and out to eat. I had forgotten how nice it was to get some guy time in and not constantly be worried if the woman you are with is thinking about someone else. Brody and I became really good friends and went out just about every weekend for a month. We typically hit the same spot since it was a street corner with about four different restaurants and bars. I began to feel a lot more confident and, as a result, I got a lot more attention from other women. I began to realize that Carly didn't have to be the only woman for me. I could be with someone who actually wanted me. As much as I hated to admit it, I was beginning to get over her.

I took Brody's advice too. Whenever Carly contacted me, I kept it brief and acted like I didn't give a flying fuck about her. It was surprisingly easy to do. I told myself that she was lucky that I even took the time to talk to her. She would constantly ask me why my conversations with her were so brief. My response was always, "You wanted to separate. We are separated."

I realize that I was being a little on the mean side, but that is what I had to do. My confidence was boosted from a sad little puppy dog to a lion. Yeah, that's right motherfucker, I win.

However, since we shared Hercules the Boxer, contact with her was mandatory, but I stonewalled her like a criminal in an interrogation room. This caused her to start asking me via text why I was always in such a hurry. I told her that it was because we weren't together anymore and I had shit to do. I also let her know that I really didn't want to be around her, which seemed to piss her off really well. After ignoring her like that for about a month, she sent me text me at one o'clock in the morning one night, drunk off her ass, wanting to bring Hercules over to my house.

"Heeeeyyy, I'm going to…um…hey. I was thinkinnnggg to bring Hercules over to your houssssee." she said. I didn't need her to even tell me she had been drinking. From the way she was slurring her words and the fact that she was even calling me at one in the morning, I knew she was drunk.

"No, it is your turn to have him and I'm in bed," I countered.

"Ugghh, fine! I'm….drunk… to drive. I can't drive… anyway," she snapped back, again making a fucking mess of the traditional sentence structure.

I knew the only reason she would even bring this up was to upset me, but it didn't work. At that point, I felt like I was over her and she had her own life completely separate from mine.

"That really isn't my problem," I said.

Then in a calm and collected voice, somewhat whimpering, she said, "You're right, I'll bring him tomorrow."

I felt so good that I was able to genuinely not care about what she was doing. I still loved her, but I had already let the relationship go in my mind.

The next day, Carly sent me another text, apologizing for her comments. She wanted to bring me a smoothie as a peace offering. She came over, and after an hour of talking about the most obscure things, she admitted that she regretted our break-up. If that wasn't sweet enough, Carly concluded her confession by asking about getting back together. Ultimately, I found that my friend's advice was the best thing I could have done to get her back, which of course, was my plan the whole time.

This kind of time apart is much more permanent than just needing a night off from each other. The freedom that I experienced during the separation affected my relationship with Carly. I found that I enjoyed being by myself sometimes. Carly and I made an agreement to spend time apart every once in a while so that we didn't drive each other crazy. This led to a biweekly girl's night out for Carly. Together with her girlfriends, she headed out to a bar, drank margaritas, and talked about everything I did that she hated. Most often, my alone time was spent going to the gym, but I made a point of getting together with my brother and my friends a lot more. If nothing else, anytime Carly went on her girl's night, I would just get some time alone, which, more often than not, resulted in her coming home and catching me with my pants around my ankles sitting at the computer.

Chapter 12: Home Sweet Home

It is a remarkable experience to meet so many different kinds of people each and every day. In the previous chapter, I wrote about how spending time away from Carly was a means of keeping our relationship healthy. When you live with somebody, however, they become an essential ingredient of the safety that your house provides from the outside world.

There is a certain trepidation that goes along with meeting new people, and this fear of the unknown really makes me appreciate the comfort I felt at home with Carly. I felt relaxed whenever I heard Carly tell me that she just wanted to sit on the couch, watch a movie, and order pizza. I didn't have to worry about crowds of people or spending money on things that weren't planned. I was able to enjoy being with somebody that I trusted, and my stresses on these types of nights were virtually non-existent. Typically we would just have our little pizza picnic, maybe a beer or two, finish up a movie and got to bed—either to go to sleep, or see if

Carly could read my mind and just get naked (This rarely happened).

Still, I needed a life outside of Carly. I normally went to the gym or drove around or window-shopped at our local department stores. It was nice to get away, have some "man-time," and relax. The only problem was that, every once in a while, I regretted leaving the comfort of home and ended up wishing I had never left Carly's side.

For example, one night I had gone to the gym and had begun my workout routine when I suddenly realized that I had forgotten my headphones. I always listen to music while working out because I absolutely can't stand to hear every muscle bound loud mouth grunting as if they were working through an anal blockage of some kind (I realize the weights are heavy, but if it causes you to grunt in order to avoid hemorrhaging, perhaps the weight is a little too heavy). So, on the one day that I forgot my headphones, it figured that the two guys on either side of me were grunting to the point of me wanting to drop free weights on their chests. These guys represented everything that annoyed me to no end. So I moved to the other side of the gym to avoid prison time and, instead, wrote them a mental note:

Dear grunting, loud, annoying gym rats,

I realize it probably feels nice, but there is no need to spread oil on yourselves before your workout. I promise that if you work hard, you will get sweaty. Consequently, as much as I love to use the bench after you have slipped off it, it makes me feel like a basted turkey. Obviously, stupidity hinders depth perception because you yell at each other as if you were across the parking lot; no one wants to hear your whole conversation. (Pssst. You are only two feet away from each other. Let's use indoor voices.)

Surely we haven't evolved from pigs, although you still grunt and snort uncontrollably because it's "helping you breathe" when I can do heavier weights and not sound like some kind of mud animal. If possible, please fix your issues before returning to the gym. Oh, and by the way, when you walk, sticking your chest out doesn't make you look bigger. It just makes you look like you are sticking your chest out.

Respectfully yours,
Annoyed gym member

While that made me feel a little better, I spotted a short butterball trying really hard to work out with the big boys. He was really getting into his music, and I heard him loudly singing off key. It was like being back at Carly's parent's family reunion. I went to another part of the gym, and as I passed him, he looked at me and just started singing as obnoxiously as possible, "Clap for 'em, yeeeaaaahhhh, clap for 'em, yeeeeeahhhhh, CLAP FOR 'EM…YEEEAAAAAAHHH."

I prayed that a roll of duct tape might appear in my pocket so that I could silence the little Sasquatch. My irritation level intensified to the point that I had to leave, but I still had to finish up my shoulder shrugs and my abdominal routine. I dug deep down for some will power and made my way over to the Smith machine. It must have been a special day, a Weight Watchers kind of day, because every single overweight person was at the gym like it was the day after New Year's. I ended up walking through a large group of overweight women wearing all white and no bras.

What the fuck?

It was like someone dropped a bag of fat tits in a white sheet on the floor and it exploded. I am surprised I didn't get hit with a fat nipple. I averted my eyes but in doing so, my gaze inadvertently landed on a midget-sized dude with lots of earrings, wearing a bright yellow Speedo. He was about to soak himself in a Jacuzzi. Vomit rushed up my esophagus and into my mouth. I forced it back down, but that was enough for me. I had to get the hell out of that gym of horrors!

Before I left, I made one last stop at the drinking fountain nearest to me. Of course, some meat head ended up walking right in front of me to take a drink first. Fine, whatever—except that he took a sip of water and just stood there. He didn't move, and I'm sure he knew I was waiting for a drink. Right before I was about to tap him on the shoulder, I heard him take a big sniff and then hock whatever lung mucus he had up into his mouth and spit it directly into the water fountain. I was appalled, enraged, and speechless all at the same time. Then, to top it all off, the fuckwit walked away like nothing happened!

"Hey! Seriously?! You hock a ball of phlegm in that thing and I am supposed to drink out of it? Why don't you also take a big shit in there while you're at it?!" I yelled.

He looked at me and shrugged, then continued to walk away while ignoring my complaint. I wanted to destroy that asshole, but ended up making a beeline straight for the exit instead.

I was sitting in my truck in the gym parking lot, trying to recover from what I had just experienced, when Carly called and asked if I could pick up a few things from Wally World. I must have said yes but I don't remember. I was still in shock from the loud-mouthed oil twins, the singing dwarf, a gay David Hasselhoff, the flying fat tits, and Captain Hock-A-Loogie. Before I realized it, however, I was circling the parking lot of the Wal-Mart, dodging people and cars until I found a parking space. No sooner did I get out of the car, some homeless dude approached me and asked for money. He claimed that he was a veteran with no arms or legs. He was wearing an army jacket that he probably got from the surplus store. He proceeded to tell me that he needed to go to the hospital because he had a bunion on his arm, which, according to his story of having no arms or legs, shouldn't have been possible. He went on to say that he didn't have a job, had no gas in his car, his children were sick with leprosy, and his wife was missing her heart. Did I mention that he was wearing a pair of two hundred dollar sunglasses? I kindly explained that all the money he needed was right there on his face. He mumbled something at me before using his phantom legs to scurry towards another shopper.

Walking into Wal-Mart offered no reprieve from meeting more circus freaks. I saw a bearded lady who weighed about six hundred pounds. She was wearing clothes that didn't fit her, and on each of her necks was a lovely tattoo. She was rolling herself down one of the aisles.

Down another aisle that was about twenty feet wide, crowds of people were gossiping to one another instead of shopping. They stood right in the middle of the aisle, preventing anyone from going around them. Lucky for me, they weren't in the aisle that I needed to visit. Carly needed salad dressing, and as I stood looking at the

50 different kinds of salad dressing on the shelves, a family of five stopped directly in front of me like I wasn't even there.

It was time to leave.

I quickly grabbed the Vinaigrette and headed towards checkout. I found one empty lane with the female cashier standing there looking bored. I walked over to her and set my item down. Not even two seconds after I did this, another cashier walked over and began talking to my cashier. They ignored me for two minutes straight. I was livid. All I needed was for this unprofessional bitch to scan one item. Finally, another cashier saw this and directed me towards her lane.

"Thanks," I said.

She began scanning my item and then suddenly stopped and blurted out, "I want your coat."

Was I being robbed? This cashier wanted my coat? Yeah, well I want a Mercedes, but that doesn't mean the next person I see driving one will give me it!

"Well, it costs $30. You can go grab one at Ross," I replied

"I didn't ask where you got it. I said that I want yours," she said. Apparently, she wasn't joking.

"Well, I hope you are strong enough to pull it off me," I offered.

"Come on, you are supposed to cut me a deal," she pleaded.

"Hey, I am the customer. You are supposed to cut me a deal, lady," I annoyingly responded.

I could not believe I was having this conversation with a cashier. So, finally, I looked at her and said, "Tell you what, you can have my coat, but only if you give me your car keys. I'll go put it in your car for you."

"Forget it, then," she said with a pissed off look in her eyes.

What world had I stumbled in to? Who were all of these people? I wondered if I was just that intolerant of people or if everyone around me just had no common courtesy. In any case, I had to leave because I would most definitely go to jail if I came across another person who pissed me off.

Regardless of whether or not it was the safety net that my home provided, my intolerance, people being people, the comfort that I felt where I could judge people from the confines of my home had never been more appreciated.

* * *

Chapter 13: Family Ties

Marriage is often accompanied by illusions of the wedding day bliss and growing old together. Most couples only think of the happy times ahead after taking their vows. Rarely, will they anticipate problems in the marriage down the road, worry about being accepted by the family they are marrying into, or consider how they will be received as a new member of that family. When you marry into a family, you are either accepted or rejected. At any point during your marriage, that acceptance can be withdrawn.

As I have said before, in-laws can have a significant effect on a relationship. When Carly married me, she knew my family as supportive and close, but it wasn't until we began having problems in our relationship that she realized the women in my family closely resemble The Mafia. She experienced butter knife death threats, drive-by spitting, and, every now and again, she would find the head of a gingerbread man with red icing on its neck in our bed.

When my family first met Carly as my girlfriend, all seemed well. They actually fell in love with her. To them, she was great. They loved that she genuinely seemed to care about me, that she took care of me when I needed it, and that she would go out of her way to do things for me. She was a wonderful change from the vile, psychotic, nasty bitches I had dated in the past. I knew how much my family liked Carly, and I knew how great that Carly was, but I still needed to transition her to be able to cope with the presence of my family. It was like training a new employee to work a printing press. Luckily, she was equipped with a very outgoing personality because, otherwise, she may have been offended by our conversations or by the eccentric habits of everyone in my family.

For example, I love my brother, Andy, and his wife. They are wonderful, but are homebodies and often refuse to leave their house. They normally decide against a typical family get-together because it would require them to leave their home. Sometimes, members of the family can take it personally, but that is just how Andy and his wife are. The less out in public they are, the better for them.

My younger sister, Becca, and my older sister, Christie, are like Paula Dean and The Barefoot Contessa. They both organize family events and make a substantial amount of food. Becca is very meticulous and organized and can put out quite a spread.

Christie is the ringleader of The Mafia. Anytime she and I get together, it is going to sound like a group of sailors stuck on an aircraft carrier. She is funny, dirty-minded, and isn't at all afraid to speak her mind or disagree with anybody. Instead of going to the movies, my family will get together with movie theater snacks to watch my sister and her husband argue. It is like watching Tina and Ike Turner with Tourettes and cerebral palsy. It is exhausting, dirty, and I love every second of it.

It only takes a glass of wine and a piece of rum cake to get my mother and sister, Christie, wasted, but once they are, nothing is off limits. One time, they got so fucking drunk together, my mother ended up wearing a lampshade, and my sister was taking pictures of her! I am pretty sure that, at one point, I caught the both of them talking to some cheese. Both conveniently deny they ever did this, claiming that I was the one who was drunk. They even allege that the whole story is some incestuous mother/sister fantasy that I've been harboring in my mind my whole life.

My dad is probably the calmest person I have met, most of the time. Every now and then he can lose his temper, but I think the reason he is so calm is because all he can do is watch the spectacle of ridiculousness that unfolds in front of him on a daily basis. He is a retired Air Force officer, and, coincidentally is my beer-drinking buddy.

...

The first time Carly came to dinner with my whole family, I had to preface to things with the possibility of a morbid and disturbing evening. I knew that I would be freakishly embarrassed by my family, and sure as shit, I was right. The topics discussed while Carly sat horrified at the dinner table included all of the following: fucking, politics, fucking, shit, shitting, bathrooms, jerking off , fucking, bodily fluids, fucking, the entire catalogue of dumb shit I have ever done in my life, and then more about fucking.

The conversation was something like this:

Christie: Hey, if he (referring to her husband) wants sex, he is going to have to just use his hand.

Me: That is so fucked up. He is your husband. When was the last time you even had sex?

Christie: I don't know, several months, but I just don't want him on top of me that long.

Me: Shit! Months? Look, let him get on top of you, pop your pinky in his asshole and be done with it.

Mom: What in the world are you all talking about?

Me: Come on, Mom, you have never stuck a finger in Dad's ass before?

Dad: Hey! Jimmy, what is wrong with you?

Christie: Bahahahahahaha!

Mom: What?! No! We did have sex under a table in a restaurant after it was closed though.

Christie (talking to me): Have you ever had anyone stick their finger in your ass?

Me: Hell no, I'm not gay. I would probably end up shitting on their finger if they did.

Mom: Well, you shit in so many other places besides the toilet. Why not on someone's finger?

With this, my moral threshold and my vomiting threshold had been reached.

Surprisingly, Carly endured our crass behavior and loved me all the more for it. I was impressed, but she still wasn't out of the family trash hole. Sometime after this first family dinner, we were invited to eat at my sister Christie's house for a light evening meal. This meant dealing with Christie's husband, Joe. I knew that if anything unexpected happened, he would get angrier than Danny Bonaduce on meth. Everything was going well until Carly reached in the cupboard for a glass and accidentally knocked over a plate. It hit the floor and shattered into pieces.

"Oh shit!" Joe yelled.

"I am so sorry. It was an accident" Carly pleaded.

"Just get out of the way! I have to clean this up before someone steps on it and sues me."

"I will pay for it. I am really sorry, Joe." She said.

"I don't need your money! Just forget about it." Joe snapped.

It was like his dead mother's urn had just split open and their dog went over and pissed in the ashes! It was a fucking plate! My mom took her aside and let her know that it was okay. It was embarrassing to break something at someone's house that you just met, but to be greeted with that kind of rage was enough to make Rocky Balboa cry. Eventually, Joe apologized for the overreaction. Joe was a serious over-reactor and seemed to have a lot of trouble in highly social settings. My family comes with a lot of people, and he really isn't amazing at dealing with more than one at a time.

•••

With most families there is always something to deal with. In my family there were a couple of things to endure, one of which is my sister's husband. More importantly, the women in my family or, The Mafia as I call them, can definitely make you feel like an outsider. Compared to The Mafia, Joe was a piece of sand in a sandbox.

My family always took my side
whenever I went through a break up. I was
always so confused about this because they
constantly teased me and made me endure
countless hours of insults and injuries
growing up. Still, it was nothing compared
to the icy cold rivers of hate that they poured
on Carly when one day during our break up,
she came to pick up Hercules. My mom, two
sisters, and my brother happened to be there
and chose not to greet her or say anything to
her. They just stared at her and made her
feel awkward and uncomfortable. It was
like they were taking her in to an empty
field and shooting at her feet just to watch
her squirm. She did squirm, too. She
couldn't escape their laser beam eyes fast
enough.

After we got back together, one of our
first conversations was about that awkward
moment. She told me that it had felt like she
had just interrupted a funeral wearing a
clown suit. I guess something was in fact
dead—my family's acceptance of her as my
girlfriend.

"Good. That is what you get for
breaking up with me," I said.

Of course, I was joking, but the look
of genuine fear in her eyes suggested she

wasn't ever going to laugh about what had happened. In fact, she had suddenly realized that no matter what I did, I would always be right in their eyes and that she would always be wrong. Always.

For instance, she and I went through a period in our marriage that I like to call, "The Dark Red Ages" (Carly has red hair). It was miserable and hard for both of us. We were constantly at each other's throats, always arguing, and it felt like I was having sex with a corpse. Nothing was sacred, not even dinnertime, as we would sometimes resort to throwing steaks and salad at each other to express how much we fucking hated living together.

I often talked to my family about the problems we had and they would instantly take my side without hearing her side. They changed their opinion of her from acceptable to MUST DIE NOW.

We were at the lowest point in our marriage—our work schedules conflicted, our bills were piled high, and we barely spoke more than one or two words to each other in a four-month period—when I decided to go and see my parents. They were living in Colorado at the time, which was about a sixteen hour drive or a two hour flight. I arrived there a few days prior to Carly, who had agreed to come after she got off work. She wasn't thrilled about coming to Colorado because of the state that our relationship was in. The minute she arrived at the house, we ended up having a huge argument. She had wanted to leave from my parent's house and go to Montana to go skiing. Skiing would have been nice, but the whole point of our trip was to be with my family in Colorado. This was the cause of our arguing.

I still cringe when I think about what happened next; my family exploded on her. My entire family had heard us arguing for two straight days, and they had had enough. My mom and both of my sisters were yelling at her, and she was yelling back.

"That is so rude! What you are doing?" Becca attacked.

"What are you talking about?" Carly inquired.

"You come in to my parent's house and are disrespectful to them and my brother! You know what? Get the fuck out. GET THE FUCK OUT OF MY HOUSE!" Becca screamed.

I haven't done anything, I am not being disrespectful!" Carly countered.

My mom and Christie chimed in, and I couldn't even hear what any of them were saying. I was stuck between a rock and a hard place because I had to either take my family's side or Carly's. Even though we were at each other's throats, I couldn't just sit there and let her be attacked.

"Don't you talk to Carly like that! What the hell is wrong with you?" I yelled.

"She treats you like shit, Jimmy, and we aren't going to just stand here and let her do it." Christie said.

"It is none of your business, and you have no idea what you are talking about!" I argued.

It was then that I realized it wasn't going to go anywhere. I was pissed at my family and pissed at Carly. What could I do except start looking online for a divorce lawyer? I was convinced that Carly wouldn't want to stay with me after my mother and sisters decimated her with their attack. Much to my amazement, they ended up making amends by the end of the visit, but it was like being on a torture rack. When your family has a vendetta against your spouse, it puts one hundred percent more strain on your relationship and can jeopardize your happiness. Just remember, in the

* * *

constipation of life, all it takes is that one extra push to break free.

Chapter 14: Understanding Women - a Guide to More Confusion

When it comes to girlfriends and wives, at one point or another, men have thought, "What the hell are they talking about?"

It's hard to believe men and women are even the same species because a woman's mind works so differently than a man's logical process. Men and women are so different in almost every area of life—from sex, to emotions and relationships, and even unimportant things like movies, TV shows and toilet paper.

My daily work schedule consisted of leaving in the early morning and not seeing Carly until I got home late at night. One night after getting off work, I walked through the door and was immediately accosted by Carly. She was in a horrible mood, snapping at me about anything and everything; my shoes were still on, I left a speck of dust on the floor, my belt wasn't lined up with my shirt. She was actually beginning to annoy me. Not only that, whenever I tried to defend myself or even attempt small talk, she seemed upset with me. I tried like hell in that moment to figure out what I could possibly have done to upset her.

Did she find out I used our account for my lunch today? Maybe I forgot to put the toilet seat down... or up? Did I leave a floater? What did I do?!

Finally, after I had been home for an hour and still getting the third degree, I asked, "What is your problem? What mortal sin have I violated to make you so upset with me?"

"You are such a jerk," she quickly barked.

"Why am I a jerk?"

"Because I dreamed that you cheated on me with some blonde chick, and when I confronted you, you pretended that you didn't know who I was!"

I laughed. So that was my offense to her? I almost couldn't believe she said this to me. Almost.

This is typical of a woman, and I should have probably just apologized and accepted her ridiculous accusation, but I couldn't remain silent. I felt that I needed to discuss what my ears were still trying to process.

"Seriously?! You are mad at me because you *dreamed* I cheated on you? You are aware that dreams aren't real, right?"

"I know, I just woke up mad at you," she said. "I can't believe you cheated on me."

Needless to say, women are VERY confusing to men.

...

Another prime example of where confusion reigns is sex. Women seem to crave the intimacy, but for men it's the physicality. This difference can be the catalyst for many arguments, the most common one being that men want to fuck way more than women. Why is this? The answer is simple: Men need the release. It's purely a plumbing issue.

Married women can sometimes request or suggest some sex, but it isn't because they want that closeness, and it isn't because they are horny. Nope. This kind of sexual conquest is because they know it has been awhile and you are going to ask anyway. So rather than be hounded about it for the next couple of days, they just want to get it over with so they can go on and enjoy their damn day.

...

Carly has confused me on so many levels. Her entire thought process confused me—I was stumped by her thinking processes when it came to sex, and I often left conversations with her thinking "What just happened?" I have studied her and tried to understand her, but nothing she did or said seemed to make any sense to me. Then one day, it hit me—the secret to why women confuse men so much is because they are like the hare moving a million miles a second, and men are like the tortoise always struggling to keep up.

Indeed, a woman's brain will fire at a pace that would embarrass most NASCAR drivers! When women speak, they are already thinking about the next thing that they are going to talk about before they are even finished talking. I remember the first time I met Carly. She spoke so fucking fast. I couldn't understand her at all! For the first month I knew her, I thought she was Russian. It took a while before I was able to understand the words coming out of her mouth. I became fluent in "Womenese."

Still, at times, I stumbled over Carly's attempts at communicating. When we first moved to Colorado, we both felt it would be exciting to travel around the state. Fortunately, there is quite a bit to do in Colorado, and it's mostly within driving distance. For our first vacation getaway in the Rocky Mountain State, we were discussing all the possible options when Carly started to become really frustrated with me because I couldn't understand what she was saying. Now, I don't exaggerate when I say she thinks so fast that when she tries to say what she's thinking, it comes out sounding like she just found a bunch of random words put together in a sentence. The conversation went something like this:

"We haven't been on a vacation for a long time," she said.

"I know, we really need to do something to get out of here and go somewhere for the weekend," I replied.

"Now that we live in Colorado, we should start doing a lot more stuff around here, and you can pretty much drive anywhere from here. They have some great packages to Mexico going on right now."

"I'm sorry, what? What are you talking about? Mexico is its own country, and it isn't in Colorado," I said.

"Yes, I know. I am just saying there are some packages that we can look at for Mexico going on right now," she replied.

"I don't get it," I told her.

"UGGHH, never mind, forget I said anything!"

"No, first you told me we should travel around Colorado, and, without pause, you said there are good deals to Mexico. Was that one thought or two collided thoughts?" I asked.

"Yes, fine, I am so sorry that I did not explain. I want to travel around Colorado. In a separate topic, there are good deals to Mexico at the moment. That's it. That is all I meant. Do you get it now?" she snapped.

"Yes, and thanks for making me feel like a third grader, while you are the one to be speaking gibberish," I said.

I had no idea what the hell she was talking about. I ended that conversation feeling like I had some sort of brain defect. We ended up going on a road trip, not to Mexico or even anywhere in Colorado. We ended up at the liquor store.

We didn't really speak for a while after that.

...

Not only are men expected to learn a new language, men are also supposed to know what a woman is talking about when she uses her code words and phrases. For example, women tell us they are okay, but they aren't. They say it is okay for us to do something, but we're assholes if we do whatever it is that we asked them permission to do. They can hold all disapproved actions over our heads for a lifetime. And, by far, the worst is when a woman thinks that she knows just about everything there is to know in this life.

One cold winter day right after New Year's Day, I started a new workout routine. It was on this day when I experienced just how much reality distortion goes on in a woman's brain. My routine consisted of weight lifting in the morning and circuit training in the afternoons, not to mention, a bitch of a diet eating cardboard and protein six times a day. Carly told me that she wanted to do it as well and that it could put us in great shape for the summer. It sounded good to me. So, I nodded my head in earnest agreement at her wanting to participate.

Carly then said in an absolutely somber tone, "I am going to do this with you, and I need your help with getting me to work out and eat better."

Any experienced married man will tell you that this is a trap and to completely ignore what she said. I wasn't experienced at all at this time, so I agreed to help her out.

Bad fucking move.

A few days later, we were eating with some friends at Guadalajara and Carly spotted their self-serving ice cream machine. She headed straight for it after we finished our meal. I immediately walked up beside her and reminded her about the vow we took to get into better shape.

"Hey, what is going on here? Do you remember our diet plan?" I reminded.

"It is just a little bit of ice cream. Don't do this in front of our friends." She threatened with an accompanied dirty look.

She was immediately defensive, and I could tell by the look she gave me that she was thinking how dare I remind her that she shouldn't eat a dessert?

Out of spite, she got an ice cream cone and filled it up while glaring at me.

"Seriously, Carly? You asked for my help, and dammit, I am going to help you," I promised.

I promptly crushed the cone while it was still in her hand so she would not be tempted by the evil dairy dessert.

"You bastard!" she yelled.

"What?! You asked me to help you. That is what I am doing!"

There was a crushed ice cream cone on the floor and cone and ice cream all over both our hands. She was looking at me in a way that I had never experienced before, and I was relatively sure I was going to die of blunt force trauma. The couple we had dinner with witnessed the entire debacle. Her good friend, one half of that couple, was just staring in awe at what I had done, while the other half, my friend, was holding back laughter as well as he could. The look in Carly's eyes told me that she wanted to cause some serious physical harm, but, fortunately for me, she chose not to.

It was then that I realized there was a more prudent avenue to get her in shape. I would simply try to explain things to her rationally and convince her to work out and eat healthier in a way that she could understand. Yeah, that would work—like slapping a murderer's hand and telling him not to kill again. While walking to the gym a few nights after the Guadalajara incident, I tried to tell her how to effectively work out. I told her what exercises to do, how many reps she needed to do, and how quickly she needed to go through them. I wasn't being bossy or mean, simply directional.

Irritated at my instructions, she stopped walking, turned towards me, and yelled, "LOOK, I DON'T NEED YOU TO TELL ME HOW TO WORK OUT, OKAY!? I KNOW EVERYTING THERE IS TO KNOW ABOUT HEALTH! "

"Well, my apologies, Almighty Ruler, I didn't know. I must not have known who I was talking to, oh Heiress of Health," I sarcastically responded.

"You just don't know when to shut up, do you?" she asked.

Apparently, explaining how to work out was not something that fell under our agreement. I didn't know what to do or say to help her, but then again, maybe it was ME that needed the help. She did, after all, know everything there was to know about health!

...

If I can just make a suggestion to all the women out there—just say what you

want to say and understand that if you have
to say it in code, or if you say one thing and
mean another, men won't understand. We
are way too stupid to read between the lines,
and unless you tell us exactly what you
mean, we will probably fuck up whatever it
is that you want us to say or do. To put it
more succinctly: explain things to us like we
are four year olds. There will be far less
conflict.

Jimmy Hyten

Chapter 15: Rats in a Cage

We take living with our parents for granted, and this is a big fucking mistake. We are in such a hurry to move out and be on our own, and then we are faced with buying toilet paper, toothpaste, paper towels, and snack foods for the first time. Likewise, having to actually pay for rent, electricity, heat, and water is also a big eye opener of just how much our parents shielded us from the harsh reality of independent living.

Once you're married, the cost of living doubles. I found that after paying these essential costs, I had very little money for much else, and our world ended up being very sad. Right after our marriage, Carly and I had bought a home and had high monthly mortgage payments. In addition to this, we also had student loans payments and an increasing credit card debt. It became so difficult that we could barely afford to live. We were mortgage poor. We were even asking homeless people for change.

Ok, that last part was a lie, but the point is that we had to do something and do it fast. We started to think about alternatives, like moving back in with our parents for instance, but the whole reason for leaving was to be on our own. After much debate, we eventually decided to cut corners, move into the smallest place we could find, and cut out all extraneous costs, such as cable, from our monthly expenses. But what would we do with our house? I decided it would be best to put our house up for rent and get the smallest apartment possible. It worked, but we slowly began to feel like we were trapped, both financially and physically. Carly and I had been used to living in a four bedroom house, and, after deciding to move out of our house, we confined our whole existence to a very small one bedroom apartment. We were rats in a cage.

Not that we didn't try to deny this fact. I kept telling Carly just how cozy and quaint things were going to be and that it was a good decision to move into the cage, er, I mean apartment. And you know what? The problems that surfaced didn't come from moving into the apartment at all. It came from Carly and I being unable to adapt to the change in scenery. If you have ever been in a small space with someone for a lengthy period of time, you know exactly what the fuck I'm talking about.

For starters, I don't think either of us dealt well with the apartment's screw-brain layout. When we walked through the front door, our living room, kitchen, and what I guess you could call a dining room (although it would be hard to dine in a space that you could only fit a folding chair in) were all overlapping into one space. There was a built-in computer desk right next to the bedroom door, which often caused blockage whenever one of us sat down in the desk chair. Juxtaposed to the desk was a midget-sized bathroom. Our bedroom was also little more than maybe three closets put together. I think capsule hotels in Japan are been bigger! Along with this, I had to stand outside the bathroom to piss. I simply couldn't fit in the bathroom. Carly found this extremely entertaining, and I suppose that, in retrospect, I did too. However, at the time, it was ultra-inconvenient. Likewise, our California king sized bed was colliding against the big screen TV in our bedroom, allowing us to only see half the screen. Talk about annoying!

After about two months of being stuck in such a small space with Carly, stupid insignificant things began bothering us, things that made not just our apartment look and feel cramped and messy, but our lives as well.

For instance, we were both reluctant to give up working together in the kitchen. I cleaned as she cooked. This had been a pretty decent arrangement ever since we met. But while trying to work side by side in a kitchen that was the size of miniature pantry, we ended up inadvertently practicing yoga and becoming pretzel people. Pots and pans clanked together, water ran everywhere, we opened the refrigerator with our feet, and turned the faucet on and off with any available body part. It was a game of Twister. And if we ever got bored of this, we would invite one or all of the dogs in the kitchen, which really made things interesting!

During one magnificent night of this kitchen chaos, Carly knelt down to find a pot she needed just as I opened the dishwasher. It smacked her in the back of the legs, taking them out and causing her to fly forward directly into the counter. In an effort to brace herself for impact, she ended up accidentally swinging at a large package of confectioner's sugar that was sitting on the counter. This then caused the sugar to go flying in my direction, ripping open as it was released from her grip. I was covered head to toe with white powder. The whole thing happened in slow motion for me. I was so stunned that I couldn't speak. Carly, who had missed the counter completely and was lying in the dishwasher, also couldn't speak.

Most people at this point would probably laugh, but what did Carly do? She fucking yelled at me about the size of the kitchen and how it was too small! Meanwhile, I was trying to wrap my brain around why I looked like a powdered donut. Our three dogs came running in to see what the commotion was and immediately began licking the sugar off me. They looked like drug dogs in a cocaine plant after helping themselves to copious amounts of powdered evidence. And I felt like a salt lick that had powdered sugar in places which should never ever have food stored inside of it!

•••

In a continuing effort to save money in this shit-hole apartment, Carly and I showered together. We saved on water and heat, but lost our sanity. Carly must be cold blooded because the second she got in the shower, she turned the water to the hottest temperature setting possible. This set off a series of events that included me barely opening the curtain and getting splashed by scalding hot water. While the flesh melted off my body, I would ask her to turn the heat down, and she will inevitably complain because it was too cold. Both of us then engaged in what I like to call "The Shower Shuffle". I would move under the faucet and she would move to the back so she could shave her legs or wash her hair. I am 6'5", so when I stood under the shower, I would have to adjust the faucet in order for the water to hit the back of my neck. But the second I moved the faucet upward, it was like a sprinkler machine gun to Carly's face.

Once we are finished with our shower shuffle, Carly washed herself with a loofah sponge similarly to the way she brushed her teeth (i.e. she scrubbed furiously, and with the amount of lather she produces, it created a nearly unavoidable soap tornado. I'd have to dodge suds left and right, the wall in the shower was full of soap, and the shower curtain was covered in soap bubbles. No matter how many times I had seen her do this, I was always amazed at her ability to clean herself. Yet, when I ask why she washed so aggressively, I never received a response.

If you were to fast forward through the rest of one of our shower experiences, I would still be screaming due to the heat, there would be more shower shuffling, I would be moving the faucet so it wouldn't hit me, Carly would be trying to duck so she wouldn't get sprayed by the faucet water, the soap tornado would get bigger, I would be reaching across her to get the shampoo, she would be reaching across me for the face soap, and finally, I would fall on her while wrapped up like a pretzel—all so we would save a little water and heat.

...

What the fuck were we thinking moving into a place that small? We thought that we were a strong enough couple to endure living in such a tiny place, but we were wrong. And the problems didn't stop with showering together. It gets way more complicated when you argue with each other in such a tiny living space. Because Carly and I had our fair share of arguments before setting foot into the Smurf mansion, our patience had been stretched so thin that all it would take was one disagreement to set shit off between us. Once that happened, forget about walking away to avoid more arguing—not in that situation. When we yelled at each other and Carly walked away, she was still right next to me. She had nowhere to go except our bedroom. Despite being entertained sometimes by her angrily stomping away, I learned the hard way that it usually meant I couldn't sleep in the bedroom and had to share the couch with our three dogs. I wasn't laughing then.

...

The last challenge we faced living in such close quarters was the issue of going to the bathroom. I'm talking about what I referred to as my poop room. Because I maintain a high protein diet and work out regularly, I tended to stink up the entire apartment when I abused my bowels. All the plants and people within a fifty yard radius would either die or suffer injuries worse than having radiation poisoning. To make matters worse, the bathroom was right next to the bedroom, similar to a closet filled with toilet paper, a commode, but no working fan to suck the putrid stench of shit safely into a hole in the ceiling.

I am a morning shitter and would normally go before Carly got out of bed. My morning routine was to wake up, use the bathroom, and head to the gym. When I would come out of that bathroom, Carly would, on cue, shoot right out of bed like I put a fresh brewed cup of coffee under her nose. It was the most effective alarm clock I have ever seen! I can still see the process unfold in every single step. I would open the bathroom door, Carly's nose would twitch, her eyes would burst open, and she would make a run for the balcony. It was glorious.

...

If you are living in a situation where you don't even have to get out of bed to use the bathroom to get off your couch or make your breakfast because your place is so small, I would suggest either relocating immediately or working out some kind of schedule between you and your significant other. Find something that will make things easier for you and your relationship. Just remember, women can be very devious, and when you abuse your bowels, they can abuse theirs. Contrary to what many of them think, women's shit doesn't smell like a flower shop.

Chapter 16: The Lost Art of Listening

There is a distinct difference between listening to someone and hearing someone. For the most part, married men know the difference between the two. There are exceptions of course. We listen, but most of the time, we either know what women are going to say before they say it, or we don't want to listen to what they are going to say. I know, I know, that's rude of me to write, but when you hear your wife nagging you day after day, you can almost predict verbatim what she'll say on a regular basis. The funny thing is that I actually listened to Carly. I paid attention and studied her because, let's face it, women still have their mysteries. They are a gender to be studied and sometimes feared. And, at least one week out of every month, they have the power to confuse the hell out of men, more so than any other week of the month.

I was no exception. When Carly had a visit from Aunt Flo, I didn't know if she was actually my life partner or a crying, yelling, bleeding, emotionally possessed gremlin. I think dealing with the waterworks every month made me realize that uncanny ability that all women possess to be either a human torch or a female Popsicle. They steal the sheets from us when we sleep and spend our hard earned money, but, at any given time, they can immediately heat up and toss all the covers right on to you and heat the entire king sized bed with their temperature. The kicker is that we love them for it. I guess it's true that most predators are nice to their prey.

...

It all started with me "not listening". Case in point: Carly's mother had recently decided to marry her long time sweetheart, and we were not only invited to attend as guests, but were also expected to be a part of the ceremony. The wedding had a Renaissance theme. This meant that I would have to dress up as a deranged musketeer. Carly knew that I would rather stick a dull spoon in my eye than dress up like a deranged musketeer.

I'm convinced a sensor went off in Carly's brain that informed her when I was doing something that made me temporarily mentally unavailable, and without fail, it was always during this time that she decided to shit on me with unfortunate news. I can even tell you when this time usually is for me: on Sunday afternoon, when I will most likely be watching football or a movie, playing Xbox, or messing around on my computer. On a Sundays, I am not at work, and, therefore, I am not required to think.

So, naturally, it was on a Sunday that Carly waited to tell me about her mother's stupid fucking wedding theme. She was in the bedroom, staring at the TV in the living room from down the hall, crouched like a cheetah, and ready to spring for her prey. I was talking to my brother via Xbox Live. Carly, seeing that I was caught up in a brutal game of Call of Duty, knew it was the perfect time to move in for the kill.

"Hey, I need to talk to you about my mom's wedding," she casually said to me, careful to not walk in front of the television screen.

"Okay, what about it?" I quickly asked.

"Well, she wants to do something different and nontraditional…not sure if you are going to like it," she hinted.

That comment should have grabbed my attention, but it didn't. My brother and I were in a team death match, and we were desperately trying to win. So, I didn't hear anything she said except for the end of what she was trying to tell me. It was something like "So, that's the theme for her wedding, it should be entertaining, and we have to dress accordingly."

I know she started and finished the conversation, but what was in the middle? Damned if I knew. Instead, I smiled and told her it sounded like fun.

Bah! What had I done? I didn't even know what I had agreed to!

A few weeks later, we were getting ready for the wedding when she handed me the clothes for the wedding. There was a clear plastic bag and all I could see was a white shirt with ruffles all over it and what looked like yoga pants. I was severely distempered to say the least!

Finally, I coughed up some words.

"Why the hell are you giving me a Halloween costume?" I asked.

"We had this discussion already, remember?"

"Hell no, I don't remember! I think I would remember agreeing to wear tights and… and whatever this shirt is," I said sternly.

She looked at me like I had just rubbed Ben Gay in her armpits.

"I told you about this weeks ago when you were playing your stupid game. You were talking to your brother and shooting Mario or whatever you were doing!!!" she yelled.

I attempted a feeble counter-attack.

"You know what! I think you knew exactly what I was doing! You told me this whole thing when I was on my game on purpose!"

She gave me a look that very clearly let me know that if I said another word, I would be castrated. I decided to save my balls and shut my mouth. And, at her mother's wedding, there I was, standing there like a gorilla who tried to fit in a child's Peter Pan costume, singing to myself, "We're men. We're men. We're men in tights!"

I think, men, there were two issues here. One was that I wasn't listening like I should have been. Like most men, I half-ass listened and then didn't get all of the information. The other issue was Carly's manipulating the situation by choosing the time that she did to tell me something she knew that I would battle her on. She did things like this quite often and dammit if it wasn't annoying. There are lots of variations of this situation with every couple. With Carly and me, it quickly led to problems.

...

What is the cure for this madness? I offer a simple solution, one that will make both husbands AND wives happy: If you want us to listen to you, offer some kind of sexual compensation. We will subsequently listen to every word that comes out of your mouth.

Chapter 17: Misery - Participation is Mandatory

There is an old expression, "misery loves company", but what if the cause of that misery is your company, otherwise known as your wife? Every marriage goes through The Dark Ages, and how long you will stay together seems to depend on how you cope with problems. Marriage is supposed to enhance and fulfill your life, but there will be times when you will get tired of your spouse and everything they do will annoy you. EVERYTHING.

Carly and I experienced a six-month period toward the end of our marriage where we were constantly at each other's throats. My stress level was through the roof, and I was more cordial to the garbage man and the trash in his truck. Well, one day during these six months, the tension between us became nuclear.

I came home from the gym to find she had cooked a steak and salad for herself and didn't prepare anything for me. We usually ate together every day. Earlier in the day, we had viciously argued about what each of us does around the house. "Was this her way of spiting me?" I wondered.

I walked in, sat down in the living room, and she immediately took a seat right next to me, her beautiful steak dinner and salad sitting on her lap. While she ate, I heard her muttering about how I will see now what she does around the house.

After that sly remark, I began listing all the shit I do around the house on a daily basis: wash the dishes, take out the trash, vacuum the house, and so on. Carly retorted by yelling at me and reminding me of all the shit that she does: cooking dinner, cleaning the dogs, making the bed, etc. We were both yelling at each other at the top of our lungs when Carly decided she'd had enough.

"When was the last time you took the trash out?" was the last thing I screamed at her before it happened.

I can still see it in slow motion. Her face had turned an unusual shade of red. I genuinely thought she was going to spontaneously combust. I looked away just in time to not see her steak flying straight towards my head. It nailed me directly on the side of my face, and then slid down my cheek and on to the floor. I couldn't fucking

My Awfully Wedded Life

believe it. She had not only thrown her dinner at me, but, more importantly, she wasted a steak! Carly's food throwing antics didn't end there. The bowl of salad was also hurled in my direction, giving new meaning to the term "tossed salad."

Furious, I began peeling the lettuce off my forehead while Oakley and Hercules quickly gobbled up the steak off the floor. Carly looked at me without any kind of grin. All I could see was raw hatred. She then stomped off towards the bedroom.

What the fuck just happened?

I gave her a little time to cool off before even attempting to talk with her. Eventually, I made my way to our bedroom where she was in bed and sulking. We then had a conversation that broke our relationship down and made us both aware of how each of us was annoyed with the other and what the problems in our relationship were. I left the room that night feeling less than satisfied with our conversation. I wasn't sure what to do, but I had an idea where it may have been headed.

Right after the steak-throwing incident, we separated for a while. Carly lived at her friend's house, and I used our reprieve from each other to promptly drink

● ● ●
167

way too much and watch break-up movies. I stayed busy as often as I could, but with the exception of eight hours of the night and the times when alcohol was soaking into my brain, thoughts of our marriage and what could happen constantly saturated my mind.

I tried to take the time apart from Carly to focus on what I truly wanted. After talking to family and friends, I came to realize that everyone has their quirks. You can't ever love every single thing about a person. Sure, Carly was hot-tempered and unpredictable, but I felt at the time, that she at least tried to take care of me. I had to realize that. So, for the time being, we decided to remain together and try to talk through our problems, while also attempting to remain productive in the relationship. Did it work? Not exactly. But, overall, I would say that Carly and I developed a stronger capacity to accept each other's faults.

When Carly returned back home, I figured out exactly when she would annoy me. Usually the potential for annoyance was the highest when we were experiencing any sort of financial hardship, when we had a rough day at work, or when we didn't see eye to eye on household chores. Thus, I avoided her in these situations as much as possible. When I was unable to avoid being annoyed by her, I let it roll off my shoulders. This seemed like it worked—up to a point.

...

It was December 2009. I was getting ready to head home from work and everything was frozen. I'm not exaggerating! I walked outside to find the building frozen, my truck frozen, and even my tires were frozen. Carly called at the exact moment that I started my car. I normally didn't mind her calling me while I was driving. I put her on speakerphone and listened. She had just come back from the grocery store and insisted on telling me about every single fucking item that was purchased. She meticulously explained to me in detail how much each item was, where she got it from, if it was on sale, the size and color, etc. You get the idea. The fact that she gave me an inventory list rather than just letting me come home and see what she bought drove me nuts. I needed a transcriber just so I could go back and see what the hell she said.

This is one area men and women completely differ. When I go to the store and buy groceries, I would tell Carly that I had picked up a few things from the store.

Carly is one of those women who need to feel like she has accomplished something no matter how big or small. Grocery shopping and coupon clipping were monumental accomplishments. I could have just walked in to our house and looked with my own eyes at what she bought. It have would be far less annoying to me. So our conversation went something like this:

"Hey, I just left the grocery store," Carly said.

"Oh good, at least we have food now," I heartily responded.

"Yeah, we will. I got a few things on sale, I bought cheese and romaine lettuce and some baguettes, and we can do something with it for breakfast, some peanut butter…"

"Yeah, that all sounds good," I interrupted. "I will look at everything when I get home."

Ignoring my interruption, Carly continued to rattle on. "…Eggs, milk, I got some flaxseed, oh and I got some fiber bars, because I know you need them too."

"Oh, thanks so much, yes, fiber bars," I sarcastically responded.

"I also got several different spices…"

"Hey!" I interjected once again. "I'm glad you went shopping. I don't need an inventory list. I will see it all when I get home."

"…Bacon, some deli meat, bread…"

While she continued to verbally assault me with a grocery list, I noticed my windshield was filthy. I doused the windshield with wiper fluid, but it was so fucking cold out that once the fluid hit my windshield, it instantly froze. I couldn't see a damn thing!

"I am going to have to call you back. I can't see anything out of my window," I said.

Completely oblivious to my peril, she asked, "What do you want to do tonight?"

"I am going to die tonight if you don't let me go, I can see nothing until I pull over and scrape my windshield!" I exclaimed.

"What time does that movie we wanted to see start tonight?"

"Carly! I have to go! I am about to hit a sign!" I yelled.

"Okay, I'll see you when you get home," she replied before promptly hanging up.

And men don't listen?

* * *

The aforementioned incident definitely annoyed the living shit out of me, but all I could do was let it go. If I hadn't, I would have driven myself crazy trying to correct her inability to stop talking to me on the phone when I needed to do something important—like saving my life.

Whether it was a grocery trip or a trip to the gas station, she had to explain everything. So, I discovered a way of amusing myself and that was to have fun with her annoying behaviors. For example, I found a loophole whenever Carly would go on and fucking on about groceries via phone: I started cross-examining her—something like this:

"Hey, I just left the grocery store; I got that cheese you like. Oh! Guess what they had on sale?" she began.

"What kind of cheese?" I quickly asked before she could launch into a full out inventory list.

"You know the stinky stuff. I think it is Bleu cheese? The sale was…"

"What kind of packaging is it in?"

"What? I don't know but I also got…"

"What are the ingredients? Because you know I only like a certain kind, Carly. It has to be that one brand of cheese."

"You know what? Forget it; I will just talk to you when I get home."

Vindicated!

Jimmy Hyten

Chapter 18: The Mistakes We Make

Can you openly admit to your mistakes? Better yet, can you realize that everything is probably your fault, or that almost anything that comes out of your mouth will most likely offend someone? If you answered yes to all of these questions, you definitely qualify for the male's role in marriage.

Most people in a marriage make mistakes, but the majority of them are made by men. Well, at least wives think this is true. Men might be aware the moment they have made a mistake, but more often than not, it takes their other half letting them know they have fucked up in some way. Some of these mistakes are forgivable, and some of them, you may never recover from. You sleep with a French, one-armed hooker one time, and they never let you live it down.

I am not talking about infidelity or dishonesty, because even a squirrel knows that these two actions are wrong. I'm talking about setting the metaphorical bar too high in your marriage, being a pushover, or saying the wrong thing to your wife. All of these things could trigger an emotional reaction in your wife, one that will involve her completely ignoring you, giving you short one-word responses, slamming things around the house, or telling you what kind of jackass you are for seemingly no reason. The kicker here is that you probably don't even know what you did to piss her off so badly!

For example, my parents have been married over forty years. I have taken notes and observed what to do and what not to do in my own marriage based on their behavior together. My dad is an excellent role model, but even he has fucked up on some unconscious level without realizing it whatsoever. My mother told me a story about when she and my dad were just married. They were preparing to go out for dinner, and she decided to get dressed up and use make-up. My mother thought it was the best make up job she had ever done, and she felt that her face looked amazing. So she asked my father if he thought she looked good.

He hesitated and looked around a little bit, then flatly said, "No, I don't like it. You look like a circus clown!"

She was shocked, offended, and started crying. How could he say such a thing to her!?

My father should've lied. If he had told her without any hesitation that she looked beautiful, no tears would've been shed. My mother would've remained happy and proud of her make-up job.

Interestingly enough, a similar situation happened between Carly and me. Carly wore this outfit that closely resembled a checker board layered on top of a stained glass window. She asked me how she looked. Instead of telling her the truth, which was something along the lines of "Wow, you look like RuPaul and Robin Hood had a child. What the hell are you thinking? Where did you even buy that? Was there a Las Vegas showgirl sale going on?" I, instead, decided to tell her "That looks good, but it would look better with different pants. The top is nice, but I really like the blue one you had on earlier."

I wasn't directly insulting her, but I was letting her know that I didn't really like the way it looked and that there were other clothes she could wear. She praised me for my opinion and appreciated that I took an active interest in her wardrobe. I didn't actually care. I just didn't want her to go out looking like a disco ball. Consequently, my father and I are alike in that we don't want our wives to be walking around looking like Mimi from the Drew Carey Show and wearing something that looks like Picasso painted it.

...

Another major mistake that men make, and I am even guilty of it myself, is setting the bar too high. This specifically applies to first impressions. When a guy meets someone that stirs him all up inside, he'll try and impress her and show the girl his very best side. For example, the girl may come over to the guy's house for the first time, and he'll make sure the place is spotless, trying hard to convince her that he isn't the raging slob that he actually is. Everything will be made to appear cozy and livable.

The problem is that when you are on your best behavior, it means that your potential love interests don't really see who you actually are inside. When she does find out what kind of a fucking piece of shit you

can be sometimes, the rest of your
relationship is spent trying to change you
back to the person she initially met. It's
fucking exhausting!

If you want a perfect example of what
I mean, consider the cleaning issue. When
you are just starting out as a couple, don't
clean your place to perfection unless that's
how it always is. Keep your place the way it
normally looks. I am not suggesting you
leave the place a complete pigsty, but no one
expects your place to look like a museum.
As your relationship progresses, you may
decide to move in together. Once she is used
to seeing your place spotless, guess what?
You'll be expected to keep it that way. What
I suggest is that if you have dishes in the
sink and underwear on the couch, leave it
there and tell her the truth, i.e., this is the
cleanest your place has ever been! Doing
this will ensure that when the two of you
move in together, she isn't wondering why
all your underwear have skid marks in them,
why you have named the family of rodents
that you consistently feed with crumbs all
over the kitchen floor, and why there are
floaters in the toilet.

There are exceptions. If you own a pet
that constantly pisses and shits on the floor,

it should probably be cleaned up. And if it's you that moves into your lover's home and you find she is the unclean one because of the family of bugs you found living under her laundry, it is best to assume she is unclean…everywhere. This would be the appropriate scenario for a break-up.

…

Living together is a breeding ground for mistakes—especially mistakes made by men. And, holy shit do women love to be right, which means that you will always make mistakes. ALWAYS.

If a woman is right about something, men won't hear the end of it. If a man is right about something, we must never tell the woman or it will end in bloodshed. It is better to just accept that men are mistake factories run by women and their home is the packaging, shipping, and receiving center for those mistakes.

I speak from experience. Carly and I tried to save money by making some of our own furniture. Our focus was mostly on a dining room table. I had the picture of what this table should look like in my mind, so I suggested she put the legs on by measuring the size of the screw and adding a piece of wood as a buffer and attaching it that way.

She stubbornly ignored my suggestion and put them on however she wanted. It may seem fairly obvious how to screw table legs to a table, but I still tried to make sure the screws didn't penetrate the surface of the table. I told her that I was familiar with penetrating surfaces, but, in this case, she wouldn't want that to happen.

She was so proud of her accomplishment. The legs were completed. There were two pieces to the legs and, each piece had four holes, making eight holes all together. However, she succeeded in fucking the table up. Rather than bracing it with an additional piece of wood underneath, which should have gone between the legs and the table to support the long screws, she just plowed them into the table. Can you see where this is headed? She was walking around strutting, showing me how little help she needed, and basically rubbing it in my face that she didn't need any of my suggestions.

In order to put the legs on, the table was upside down. We turned the table over to test the stability of the legs and all eight screws were popping out of the newly finished surface of the table. We both laughed hysterically.

"I guess we can stick some candles on them," I suggested.

"Or use them as hot plates?" she added.

Now, I could've told her that if she had only listened to me, we wouldn't have had this problem to begin with. But saying this would've also meant that I would've never heard the end of it either. It could've become an all-day argument festival and ruined our time together. However, I can guarantee that if it would've been me who made that same mistake and Carly was the one who had suggested the correct way, she would have repeatedly reminded me about my ignorance of her indiscretion.

...

I was not perfect when it came to listening to Carly, but a rhetorical question that I heard on a daily basis from her was "When are you going to learn to just listen to me?"

Ugggghhhhh!

Why did I hear this all the time? Because Carly thought that she was right about everything (as most women do). So I did my best to let her think she was always right because it was easier for me to avoid having a conversation about her being Stephen Hawking incarnate!

There were times, however, that pointing out her mistakes was unavoidable. Carly typically did the budget. She was organized and careful. It made sense for her to be in charge of this important task. She would write all of the amounts allocated for each of our expenses on a sheet of paper. For example, we designated money for gas each pay period. During one particular week, she told me that I had $40 to spend on gas. You see, I remember details very well. I knew what she had said. So, I went to the gas station and spent exactly $40. A few days went by, and we were sitting at my parents' dinner table with Sara, a mutual friend, and my dad. Carly was on their computer and happened to check our bank account. She saw the gas charge and instantly was all over my case for spending the $40 because she said I should only have spent $30. By her reaction, you'd have thought I had started WW III. Knowing exactly what she had said, I countered back. We argued for at least ten minutes straight. Sara and my father must have felt really awkward, but I didn't care. I wanted to prove how completely fucking wrong she was about the matter. She came back to sit at the table and had her arms crossed the whole time. Anytime we made eye contact, she instantly gave me the evil eye.

On the way home from my parent's house, we erupted. I kept trying to explain my side, but she wouldn't believe me. We argued right until we walked in the front door. She went over to our computer desk and picked up a piece of paper that had the allocated amounts.

"Oh, wow, it looks like I did tell you $40," Carly quietly said.

"I know that is what you said! That is what I have been trying to tell you!" I shouted.

"I could have sworn I told you it was going to be $30."

"Call my dad and call Sara and tell them you were wrong. You are not living this one down," I demanded.

"I'll call them. I loathe you." She surprisingly agreed.

She stayed pissed the rest of the day, but not because of our argument. It was because I proved her wrong.

...

It's important to mention that there are different levels of mistakes. You can point out a mistake like the aforementioned one and have your wife be upset with you for doing it, or you can point out little funny mistakes that could result in laughter and good times.

I was in the kitchen eating oatmeal one morning while Carly was getting ready to leave for work. I was sitting on the counter, teasing the dogs with my food. Carly scampered around the house, frantically trying to get ready. At some point she screamed from the back room, "Hey, babe, have you seen my black belly fat?"

I spat my oatmeal all over the dogs. Not only did I not know what the fuck she was talking about, but if she had asked if I had seen any fat anywhere, I would have instantly denied it.

"What the hell did you just say?" I asked, trying not to laugh.

She came into the kitchen and asked, "Have you seen my black ballet flats?"

Oh, you weren't looking for belly fat, but ballet flats. Riiiiiigghhht.

She initially spoke so quickly that I grossly misinterpreted her—fucking amazing. I told her what I thought she said and she broke into hysterical laughter. This kind of mistake is okay to discuss, but be careful. If you bring up a mistake that isn't minor or amusing, you may end up with black belly fat from getting gut-punched by your significant other.

...

The key to avoiding bodily injury and not permanently pissing your wife off is to find a middle ground. If you have to ask yourself if something is going to bother her, it will! And no matter what the situation is, women want to feel special. I'm not suggesting you should be a pushover, but don't just point out every mistake that she makes either. Tell her the truth without being a dick about it. You can also lie to keep the peace, if necessary, and remember this most of all: don't bite the hand that feeds you…or the one that takes off your clothes.

Chapter 19: The Devil Has Double D's

Every marriage comes to a fork in the road. It's that time when a husband, or wife, or both feel like their differences are irreconcilable. A decision has to be made. Do you stay together and figure shit out, or do you split up? No matter what kind of person you are or how strong your relationship is, there will always be temptation, doubt, uncertainty, heartache and pain. Hence, the common popular saying, "The grass is always greener on the other side of the fence," I believe is open for interpretation. That other side may have patches of green grass, but in my experience, it is mostly a field of dead grass that only looks appealing from a distance.

It's easy for me to look back in retrospect and wish I had done something differently about the demise of my marriage to Carly. It's easy to pity myself and wish that I had made better choices in my marriage, but the fact is, I hadn't. I made a terrible mistake that I will regret the rest of my life. I'm only writing about it now because it was the awful conclusion to three and a half years of a marriage that was filled with fighting and mutual disrespect.

I had just started a job being the office manager for a mortgage fraud company. For the first time in two and a half years of marriage, things seemed good. We weren't having problems, and we finally seemed to be settling into a healthy relationship and routine. Along with this, I was finally doing something that I had wanted to be doing for a living, and I was beginning to get recognition for my work. I was hearing a lot of praise from people, and there was one in particular who would always make a point of telling me how good of a job I was doing. Her name was Beth and she was someone who, despite me being married, made a point of constantly flirting with me. I would be lying if I wrote that I didn't flirt right back. How could I not? She had long dark hair, beautiful fake tits, and was 6'1 in heels. She definitely stood out. Still, I saw her only as a very attractive friend.

I wasn't sure if Beth knew I was married. I wore my wedding band, but sometimes people don't pay that close attention. I say that very naively, but women who are interested in men definitely notice a wedding ring. Perhaps Beth noticed, or maybe she didn't, but whatever the case was, it didn't stop her from wanting to exchange emails with me. Our conversations were innocent and mostly the usual information-collecting kind. She wanted to know about me, and I was curious about her as well. But, I had to somehow get the message to her that I did, in fact, have a wife. So, in an email, I told her very nonchalantly something I had done the previous weekend with Carly. She responded with asking how long I had been married and telling me she had thought my wedding band was a "scare-off girls ring."

If it would have been possible to hear her inflection, her email might have sounded as if she was extremely disappointed. I kept telling myself that no matter how attractive she was, I was devoted to Carly and would never let anything happen. Beth and I exchanged emails multiple times throughout every day and then it happened: Beth asked me if we could hang out together outside of work, alone, and if Carly would mind this at all. *Yeah, I'm absolutely sure that Carly would be fine with me leaving her on some weekend to go hang out with a beautiful surgically enhanced woman! She would be fine with that like the Pope would be fine having lunch with Hitler!* Still, I had to try, right?

I casually brought it up to Carly that I had a friend at work who wanted to hang out with me. I told her that this friend was a woman and that she just seemed like someone who may be fun to hang out with. Just as casually as I had brought it up, she dismissed it with a chipmunk laugh. Carly wasn't cool with the idea? No real surprise there.

Beth and I continued to email each other. If I had a free second at work, I would go over to her desk to bullshit. She reciprocated. Eventually, we would take walks around the office building and talk about everything and anything that came to our minds. I didn't feel like I was doing anything wrong because we were only acting like life-long friends.

One afternoon, I asked Beth if she wanted to go for a walk because I was having some trouble at home. She more than happily agreed to take a walk. I explained to her that Carly and I had another argument about finances. Beth listened astutely and seemed interested in every word flying out of my mouth (I realize now that there was another reason she was staring so hard at my lips when I was speaking), and this encouraged me to fucking spill my guts to her. I told her EVERYTHING that was wrong with my marriage. It was like all of the pent up negative feelings that I had harbored about Carly refused to be hidden away inside of me anymore. Beth didn't say a word throughout my entire rant, which probably took about twenty minutes. When I was finally done, she shot me a devilish grin and said something which I'll never forget:

"Jimmy, if we were together, I would love you better than anyone has ever loved you in your life."

I should've stopped her, but I was too stunned. What could I say? I wasn't expecting that at all. Or maybe I was, I dunno. But, it didn't stop there. Beth took my silence as her cue to let all of her feelings about out into the open. She told me about how great our relationship would be, how she would never treat me like Carly did, and promised me that we would fuck like crazy. Beth looked me dead in the eyes, and with that devilish grin still on her face, she went on to tell me that she would be sexually willing to do anything and everything. She then went into specifics:

She loved giving blow jobs, she loved anal, and that she would be more than willing to fulfill every fantasy that I had ever had.

This should have been a red flag to me. This kind of thing only happens in porn movies. There I was, a married man, and this woman was telling me that she loved to wear no underwear and have sex outside in public. Despite this, I didn't stop listening to her words. Long after I got home that day from work, I continued to listen over and over again in my mind to her dirty promises.

Throughout the next few weeks, the flirting got heavier and heavier. I soon convinced myself that I was with the wrong person. We continued taking walks around the building. The walks got longer and longer, and the talks became more promising. One afternoon, I was at her desk, just talking, when she told me she was wearing her very low cut top just for me. She then moved her shirt and exposed one of her breasts. This both interested me and disappointed me. What was I doing? I was married and she knew it.

My relationship with Carly began to suffer. One day, she just stopped talking to me altogether. We had a minor disagreement, and from that point on, we didn't speak to each other. The third day of not speaking, I wondered if maybe she was feeling what I was feeling, that perhaps our marriage was over. I meant to leave from work early that third day and talk to Carly about everything, but on my way out the door, Beth talked me into taking another walk with her to talk about what was happening at home.

We ended up sitting on the grass near our work building for about two hours. Midway through our conversation, she moved closer to me and begged me to kiss her. I refused, citing the very marriage I was complaining about. Beth saw how weak that defense wall was and kept inching closer and closer until she was pretty much in my lap. She continued to offer me the world, and sex, and a better relationship filled with understanding and beauty and roses and angels.

Fuck it. I kissed her.

It wasn't a quick kiss either, but a slow, passionate, lip-melting, dick-hardening kiss.

What had I done? I was married and I had kissed another woman.

Beth then began hinting at how fun it would be if we just fucked right there. That wasn't me and I knew better. I left immediately, ashamed of what had happened.

Carly and I approached the fifth day of not talking to each other. Maybe she wanted out but didn't know how to tell me. I think that is always the "guy's" way out; if we want to break up, we try to have the girl initiate it. I told my family how I was feeling about the whole situation and they were on board with my decision to break things off with Carly. They had seen the problems we had had in the past and knew that our marriage wasn't going to last.

My sister invited everyone over to her house for dinner that fifth night. Carly refused to come because of whatever the fuck was going on between us, so I invited Beth instead.

What in the world was I thinking? Here I am, still married, and inviting this other woman over to meet my family. My moral compass appeared to be broken. Beth arrived at my sister's, with a little surprise: her 5-year old daughter. I wasn't exactly sure how to process that.

After a few drinks with my family, Beth made a good first impression on everyone. Her daughter was also a hit with my family. By the end of the evening, I decided that Beth was exactly what I wanted. My marriage was over.

Carly called me that night, during dinner to be precise, and begged me to come and talk with her about our marriage. I refused and told her we would have to talk later.

She kept pressing the matter until finally I said, "I am just done with us."

"What are you talking about?" she asked.

"I am just tired of this shit with you, and I am done with it. I don't want us anymore," I explained.

What was I saying? I couldn't believe what was coming out of my mouth. I had more history with this woman than anyone else. I had chosen to spend my life with her and, there I was, pushing for a divorce?

"I am going to get on a plane to Houston tomorrow unless you tell me not to go," Carly said.

"I think you should go then." I responded.

Despite feeling like shit about it, I convinced myself that not being with Carly was the best thing for me. I had the support from Beth the whole time, telling me it was the right decision and how wonderful things were going to be from then on.

It took a couple of weeks to be okay with everything that happened. Carly moved out of our house and was living with a mutual friend. At last, I was free to start dating Beth.

On our second date, Beth came back to my house. Because of the soon-to-be divorce, I was living with my parents on the bottom floor of their house. Neither Carly nor I wanted to stay at our old place. Beth brought her daughter, which was fine with me, and we talked with my family all night. She stayed so late that everyone started going to bed while she was still there. I was tired as well and told her I was going to bed and, if she wanted, she could keep talking to my family. Beth decided to call it a night as well. She put her daughter to sleep in my parent's guest bedroom and then came to bed with me. That raised another very red flag. We had just finished our second date, and Beth jumped into my bed wearing nothing but red lace underwear. I let it go because I couldn't see past the desire.

I had hoped to be considered a different kind of man, but when it came to a gorgeous, nearly naked woman lying in my bed, I acted no different than any other man would have in that situation. I wish I could say that I realized the error of my ways and that I would have told her to put her clothes on and leave, but the truth of the matter was that we screwed like crazy that night, all night. It was the first of many sleepless all-night bang sessions with Beth.

I hated how things ended with Carly and hated even more that I could be influenced by a naked body, plastic surgery, and empty promises. I tried to move on, keep the new relationship with Beth in good condition, and tried, most of all, to not think about what I had left behind. It seemed as though the grass was, in fact, greener on the other side.

Carly still pleaded with me to get back together. I tried to feel nothing, and things seemed actually peaceful for a change in my life.

•••

A couple months had gone by since Carly and I had split up, and I had agreed to meet with her so she could spend some time with our dogs. We also needed to discuss the legal matters that needed to be addressed with getting divorced. We met at a public park. Carly was upset that I hadn't shown one ounce of emotion through this whole thing. Thank God I was wearing sunglasses because my eyes filled with tears.

"If you haven't already, you will regret your decision," she said very firmly.

I didn't say anything in return. I did regret my decision. I wanted us back more than anything, and I still couldn't believe what I had done. But, at the same time, there was also a peace in my life that I hadn't had since…well, since before I got married.

Unfortunately, that peace didn't last. The next few months were very difficult because my relationship with Beth became very hot and cold. I didn't show any interest in her until she started talking about sex or got naked. I was having trouble balancing what my body wanted and what my heart wanted.

If I can backtrack a little bit, there is one very important detail I left out about Beth's daughter. If there was a picture of her with a description below it, it would say she was spawned from Satan's loins. She was the worst behaved child that I had ever met in my life. There was no measure to the insanity that fucking demon child eventually brought into my life. Beth was sleeping over practically every night, and she set up a cot for her daughter in my room. My parents didn't want her occupying the guest room all the time. The child woke up all throughout the night, crying and screaming about wanting candy, or wanting this, or wanting that. I was ready to kill myself.

In addition to this, my part of the house was flooded with her toys. The fucking kid would also leave food everywhere and not put dirty plates in the kitchen sink. Beth didn't do anything to correct her either. I kept telling myself that "I can't do this." I didn't want to be a parent, but the only thing that I could do was to look past it and hope that I could get used to having a child around.

Despite being hot and cold with Beth, things seemed to be mostly okay between us, except for the fact that I was very unsure of what I had done. I was still preoccupied with the hurt and pain I felt from leaving Carly after seven years. I was hoping what I had done would be worth it.

•••

As far as Beth was concerned, our relationship lasted about four months, and it developed faster than I could ever have wanted it to. After only two months, she asked me to adopt her demon spawn of a child and get married, which scared me to death. The chaos with her daughter's behavior and the craziness that Beth seemed to harbor became overwhelming. In addition to becoming very good friends with Mr. Crown Royal, I realized I hadn't ended my marriage to be so unhappy with someone else. Beth and I split up, and I'll be okay if I never talk to or see her again.

Carly never knew about Beth or any of the events that unfolded leading up to the end of our marriage. I have to give credit to Carly. Because of our marriage, I learned so much about myself and the kind of relationship that I want. It wasn't until the end when I realized that my feelings toward Carly weren't what they should have been for a married couple. In order for either of us to have had a chance at happiness, I had to officially end it.

Epilogue

You have just read about the last eight years of my life. Marriage was a concept that didn't play out well for me, so I had committed myself to never making that mistake again. It wasn't until this past year and a half that I began thinking differently. Throughout the whole Beth ordeal and through the divorce from Carly, I had a friend who was always very supportive and comforting. There were never any romantic feelings involved until one day there were. Her name is Jackie, and my friendship with her has evolved into a romance. She is the grass that is greener on the other side; I just wasn't able to see it until now. In her, I have found my best friend and someone who I can honestly say is the absolute love of my life. She fulfills my every need and want. And after my last two relationships, I am convinced that she was the one I had been looking for all along. We're married now and I'm confident that my marriage to

Jackie is a real honest to God marriage.
Warts and all.

When I began writing this book, I
didn't anticipate that it would end with me
being divorced, or that I was going to end up
on one side of the fifty-percent divorce rate.
The whole reason I began this venture was
because I was upset about an argument I had
with my ex-wife and I thought, "How do
men do this? How is it that we can never
win an argument and are always wrong?"

I knew that I shared this frustration
with many men, one of which is my dad. I
grew up witnessing my parent's marriage. It
was a healthy one, but still, there were some
consistencies I saw in their marriage, in my
sister's marriage too, and my brother's
marriage, and my own marriage. The bottom
line is that men and women are different.
We think differently, act and react
differently, and are often intrigued by each
other's gender. We may not understand our
differences, but it's these differences that
drive us to do the things we do.

So whether you're a man or a woman,
I want anyone who is in a relationship to
read these stories and think, "We go through
and deal with the same thing!" The bottom
line is that we are all flawed human beings

that marry, divorce, cheat, and embarrass each other. But, we also have a tremendous capacity for loving each other as well. We should be loyal to those who truly make us happy, even if it takes a couple of tries. No matter what though, you gotta take a step back and find humor in everything you do together and in everything around you too. Like gnomes.

Jimmy Hyten

About The Author

Jimmy Hyten lives in Denver with his wife
and pets. He is a freelance writer and works
for the Department of Public Safety. He
considers himself a family man and an
exercise nut as well. Although he barely
survived his first marriage, Jimmy now
considers himself a reborn husband who is
completely devoted to his significant other,
body and soul.

Jimmy Hyten

My Awfully Wedded Life